The Official

MET

Practice Test
Book

with Answers

 MICHIGAN LANGUAGE ASSESSMENT

University of Michigan Press
Ann Arbor

ISBN-13: 978-0-472-03762-9

2022   2021   2020   2019   4   3   2   1

CONTENTS

Introduction
for the Student

The Official MET Practice Test Book with Answers contains four full versions of the test. These practice materials will give you an idea of what the test is like as you prepare to take the actual exam. In addition, the book includes the accompanying answer keys and audioscripts for each of the four practice tests, as well as a Progress Tracking Log and selected vocabulary lists from the practice tests, so it is ideally suited to self-study. We suggest planning to take all four practice tests and scheduling plenty of time in between each test for additional study and review. Taking the practice test multiple times will increase your confidence and help you decide where to focus your additional study efforts based on your individual results.

These practice tests are approved by Michigan Language Assessment; they are meant to be used along with or at the conclusion of a regular course of English study or review as you prepare yourself for the MET. Practice tests are only one component of an effective test-preparation program and must be administered in accordance with the guidelines provided to be most useful. With continued study, including test practice and carefully scheduled targeted follow-up study and review, you can expect to improve your chances of performing well on the MET. Please note, however, that obtaining a high score on any of these practice tests does not guarantee a high score on the actual exam.

This book of practice tests provides an opportunity to simulate an actual MET, including both the multiple choice Listening and Reading sections and the optional Writing and Speaking tests. All the test items have been developed by Michigan Language Assessment and correspond in content, form, length, and difficulty to an official test. There are some minor differences in the way the test is presented in this practice test book compared to the test booklet; however, none of these differences should affect a test-taker's performance on the test. In addition, for the Listening section, there are some minor differences in the audio instructions provided; a student or teacher may choose to pause the audio recording between the different parts of the Listening test, whereas on the actual test, there is no pause between each part.

For the Writing and Speaking tests, the book is both a preparation aid as well as an opportunity to practice the writing and speaking tasks under timed conditions. Each practice test in this book has a corresponding set of writing prompts that have been specifically selected to go with a specific practice test.

There are four sets of Speaking prompts in a separate section of this book. These prompts are not necessarily paired with a specific practice test because during the actual administration of the speaking test, the examiner can choose from several available speaking prompts. A range of possible similar prompts is included in this book.

Introduction
for the Instructor

The Official MET Practice Test Book with Answers is your official teacher's version of the practice test book for the MET. Your students will be using the Classroom Edition of *The Official MET Practice Test Book*. This book contains the full text of all four practice tests and the speaking test prompts provided in the Classroom Edition, plus a Progress Tracking Log and selected vocabulary lists from the practice tests. It also contains answer keys for each test, audioscripts for the Listening sections, suggested answers to the sample written responses for Tests 1 and 2, and the examiner instructions and script for the Speaking test.

Because the practice tests are approved by Michigan Language Assessment, you can be assured that your students are receiving the most relevant targeted test preparation available for the MET. Practice tests are only one component of an effective test-preparation program and must be administered in accordance with the guidelines provided in order to be most useful. Please note, however, that obtaining a high score on any of these practice tests does not guarantee a high score on the actual exam. With continued study, including test practice scheduled with targeted additional study and review, students can be expected to improve their chances of performing well on the MET.

This introductory section provides a detailed overview of the test, information about how to use this book, including specific suggested strategies for the most effective test-taking practice, and instructions for scoring and interpreting the practice tests.

Introduction
to the Michigan English Test (MET)

The MET is a standardized international examination designed by Michigan Language Assessment (MLA), aimed at upper-beginner to advanced levels—A2 to C1 of the Common European Framework of Reference for Languages (CEFR). It assesses general English language proficiency in educational, social, and workplace contexts.

The MET can be taken as a two-skills or four-skills test. The Listening and Reading sections are required; test-takers can choose to take the optional Writing and Speaking sections. The test emphasizes the ability of the test-taker to communicate effectively in English. Listening recordings and reading passages reflect authentic, everyday interaction in an American-English linguistic environment. Grammar and vocabulary are included in the Listening and Reading sections.

The MET is intended for adults and adolescents at or above a secondary level of education who want to measure their general English language proficiency in a variety of linguistic contexts. The test results can be used for educational purposes, such as when finishing an English language course, or for employment purposes, like applying for a job or pursuing a promotion that requires an English language qualification. The MET may also be used as a bridge to a higher proficiency–level exam, such as the ECPE. There is no pass or fail on the test; it is a multi-level exam covering a range of proficiency levels from A2 to C1 on the CEFR.

Format and Content of the Test

The MET is a paper-and-pencil test with 100 multiple choice questions in two required sections: I: Listening and II: Reading and Grammar. **The total time allowed for the multiple choice portion of the test is 100 minutes.**

The optional portion of the test includes a 45-minute Writing section, which is taken at the same time as Sections I and II, and a 10-minute Speaking test, which is scheduled separately.

The content of the MET reflects a range of situations likely to be familiar to most test-takers, focusing on the public, educational, and occupational domains, with an emphasis on topics from the educational domains.

The four components to the MET are outlined in this chart.

Section 1: Listening	35 minutes
Part 1: 19 short conversations between two people	19 questions
Part 2: 4 longer conversations between two people	14 questions
Part 3: 4 short talks	17 questions
Section 2: Reading/Grammar	**65 minutes**
Grammar	20 questions
2 extended reading passages	10 questions
2 sets of thematically linked reading passages	20 questions
OPTIONAL SECTIONS	
Section 3: Writing	**45 minutes**
Task 1: 3 questions on a related theme	
Task 2: 1 extended essay response	
Speaking Test	**10 minutes**
Part 1: 3 short questions (60 seconds allowed for each response)	
Part 2: 2 tasks (90 seconds allowed for each response)	

Listening

This Listening section of the test consists of three parts with a total of 50 questions. The first two parts are based on conversations. Part 1 includes short conversations between two people with one question per conversation. Part 2 includes six longer conversations between two speakers with two to four questions per conversation. Part 3 is four short talks with three to five questions per talk. The format of the questions is multiple choice with four answer choices. The question and answer choices are printed in the book (or test booklet). Candidates hear the recording and the questions only once; they answer the questions as they listen. Once the audio for the Listening test has started, it will not stop; it will play continuously and include pauses to allow time to answer the questions.

Reading

The Reading section consists of three parts with 50 questions. Part 1 consists of 20 questions on a variety of grammar structures with a majority of the topics focusing on the academic domain. Part 2 includes two extended reading passages about a range of academic or general topics and has five questions for each passage. Part 3 includes two sets of three longer texts on a related theme. The texts are on topics of general interest. All questions are multiple choice and have four answer choices. Questions and answer choices are printed in the book.

Writing

The Writing test requires test-takers to answer questions in writing at the sentence level and the paragraph level and to produce a short essay in response to a single prompt. Task 1 includes three short questions that can be answered in a few sentences or a short paragraph. The writing tasks are progressively more difficult. The final longer essay task (Task 2) demands a response of one to two paragraphs and a higher level of skill. Students write their answers in the book.

Speaking

The Speaking test is a structured, one-on-one interaction between an examiner and the test-taker that consists of two parts and five distinct tasks. The tasks in Part 1 require test-takers to convey information about a picture and a similar personal experience and to then give a supported opinion on a related topic. The two tasks in Part 2 involve explaining the advantages and disadvantages of a particular idea or proposal and taking a position on another topic and trying to convince the examiner to agree with their idea. The Speaking test is taken separately from the other parts of the test.

This practice test book with answers contains answer keys, audioscripts, and accompanying sample writing responses with commentary. These practice materials with answers are provided for teachers whose students are using the Classroom Edition of the practice test book and also offer English language learners the opportunity for self-study outside of a class or formal test-preparation program.

The Official MET Practice Test Book with Answers includes:

- 4 complete practice tests
- 4 sets of practice Speaking test prompts
- information on accessing the audio (MP3) files
- a progress tracking log for recording practice test scores
- selected practice test vocabulary lists
- answer keys
- audio transcripts for the Listening tests
- sample Writing Test responses with commentary for Tests 1 and 2
- the examiner instructions and script for the Speaking test
- actual test instructions and a sample answer sheet

Suggested Practice Strategies

Scheduling of Practice Tests and Review

Each practice test should be taken under the same conditions by following the exam administration procedures provided in this book. Teachers or test-takers should then mark the exam and schedule additional study and review according to the specific results of each practice test.

The four practice tests in this book are equivalent in difficulty and may be taken in any order. For best results, take the first practice test at the beginning of the course or semester in which you will be taking the exam. Score the test immediately and study your results. For teachers: Further classroom study can be tailored according to the needs of the class as a whole, with suggestions for individualized study and review based on each students' performance. In the middle of the semester or course term, or after at least six to eight weeks of additional study and review, the second practice test can be taken. Again, further study and review should be planned based on results and improvement from the first to the second practice test. Finally, the last two tests can be taken closer to the date of the actual exam, again with ample study time in between.

For an accelerated practice test schedule, either for independent study or in a classroom setting, it is suggested that you allow at least one week in between practice tests, with intensive, targeted study and review based on the sections of the test needing the most improvement. Without sufficient practice and review time in between practice tests, significant improvement in scores is unlikely. Memorization of specific test questions is not recommended, and familiarization with the topics, format, and timing of the test—while helpful—is not sufficient as a test-preparation strategy without additional study.

Listening and Reading and Grammar: Review Your Mistakes

- Whenever you take a practice test, study all your incorrect answers and make sure you understand the correct answer. Your errors will help you know what you need to study.

- If you guessed at an answer and got it right, review those items to confirm your guesses.

- Track your scores using the Progress Tracking Log. Record key vocabulary and other things you want to remember to do on the next practice test or the actual text. For example, you may want to note listening or reading items missed or vocabulary or grammatical structures that you were unsure of and organize them in a way that helps you review them.

Writing and Speaking: Get Expert Help

- For the Writing and Speaking tests, make sure you have a qualified teacher, tutor, or expert English user review your responses and give recommendations and suggestions for improvement. Although it will not be possible to accurately score your speaking or writing practice test, the scoring criteria are available online (www.michiganassessment.org), and your teacher can help you understand how your response compares to the sample responses and scoring criteria.

- Set specific goals for additional speaking and writing practice based on this feedback.

- Record vocabulary, notes, or outlines of the topics you want to remember to help to prepare you for the next practice test or the actual text.

Practice Good Test-Taking Strategies

- Learn how to eliminate wrong answers and narrow down your choices for multiple choice questions.

- Practice taking notes while listening to the audio passages.

- Practice reading and answering questions with a time limit by using a stopwatch.

The MET is used for a variety of purposes at different proficiency levels. Some test-takers take the MET before they have reached a level of proficiency suitable for their intended use of the test. We hope this practice test book helps test-takers to better judge their preparedness for the exam and to target additional study activities based on the results of each practice test.

Administering the Practice Test

It is important to take the practice test under proper test conditions. You should take it in a place with a table and chair that is quiet and free from distractions. For the two-skills version (Listening/Reading only), allow approximately 1 hour and 45 minutes of uninterrupted time. For the four-skills version of the test, the Listening, Reading, and Writing sections are administered in one sitting without a break. For the most realistic practice, please allow 2 hours and 30 minutes of uninterrupted time for these three sections. The 10-minute practice Speaking test is administered separately on the same day or within a few days before or after the written test.

When you take a practice test, follow these steps:

1. Gather all of the test materials:

   a. the **practice test book**

   b. a **device on which to play the audio (MP3) files** for the Listening sections, which can be found at www.press.umich.edu/elt/compsite/met

   c. **pencils**

   d. a **timing device** such as a clock or stopwatch.

2. Turn to the instructions for **Section I: Listening.** Start the Listening Section audio recording. Once you start the audio recording, do not pause it or stop it. By using the time permitted on the recording, you will get practice listening and responding in the set amount of time. **The entire Listening section will last about 35 minutes.**

3. Mark your answer to each question directly in the book. The audio includes a pause after each question so that you can mark your answer immediately after hearing each item. Once the audio recording has finished, do not replay it or change your answers. Move on to Section II immediately.

4. Read the instructions to **Section II: Reading and Grammar. You will have 65 minutes for this section of the test.** When you have finished reading the instructions, note the time you are starting this section and the time you must stop working on it. Then begin answering the questions in Section II. Mark your answers directly in this book. You may go back to review your answers in the Reading Section as long as you have time remaining.

5. Stop working after 65 minutes. Do not change any of your answers after the 65 minutes of test time for this section is over.

6. Follow the instructions for each section of the Writing test. **Allow for an additional 45 minutes**. Note the start time and stop writing after 45 minutes. You should complete the writing tasks in the order they are given because they are progressively more difficult. Part 1 of the Writing test should take less than half of the 45 minutes; Part 2 requires a longer response so plan for more time to complete this task.

7. Refer to page 184 for the Speaking test instructions. The practice Speaking test must be given by a proficient language teacher or expert English user who will read and follow the examiner instructions and script in the book (pp. 185–188), while the students look at the illustration and questions provided in the test portion of the practice test book (pp. 117–124). (In the Classroom Edition, the pages are 111–118.) The test should be conducted in a quiet, one-on-one, face-to-face setting. For the best practice and review opportunities after the test, the entire Speaking test should be recorded (as it will be on test day), either on a device supplied by the instructor or on the student's own device.

Scoring and Interpreting Your Test

Scoring the Test

When students have finished taking Sections I and II of the practice test, they should have a completed practice test with one answer per question. Teachers will need to decide how to score students' practice tests. Depending on the students' ages and your time constraints, you may want to provide the answer key to the class and either ask students to exchange books and score a partner's exam or ask them score their own exams. Or, if time permits, you can collect the books and score them yourself. Please follow these steps to score the multiple choice section answers.

1. Compare answers with the corresponding answer key for each practice test. If the answer matches the answer key, then award one point. Please note that if more than one answer is marked to a single question, no point is earned.

2. Add up all of your correct answers in Section I: Listening. This is your Listening score. Record it in the Progress Log.

3. Add up all of your correct answers in Section II: Reading and Grammar. This is your Reading and Grammar score. Record it in the Progress Log.

4. Make notes in the Progress Log about vocabulary and grammar items you want to remember or study further.

5. The next section explains how your scores on the practice test may be interpreted in terms of MET scaled scores, which are the official MET scores.

Interpreting Your Scores

This section provides information helpful to understanding how your performance on the MET practice test is related to how you might perform on an official MET.

The MET is a multi-level exam, covering a range of proficiency levels from upper-beginner (CEFR level A2) to advanced (CEFR level C1). There is no pass score, but the emphasis of the MET is on the middle of the range (B1 and B2). The exact cut scores between adjacent CEFR levels, based on research conducted by MLA, are available on our website, where selected CEFR performance descriptors illustrate what test-takers should be able to do at each level. It is important to note that the score ranges for the CEFR levels are provided for each section but not for the final score because it is possible for an examinee to be at a higher language proficiency level in one language skill than in another. Therefore, all section scores should be taken into account when interpreting the test results for use in decision-making.

When the MET is taken under examination conditions, the raw scores from Sections I and II are converted to scaled scores, which relate to particular CEFR levels. This method ensures that the language ability required to receive a scaled score remains the same from year to year and that scores on all MET forms are comparable. The MET practice test is designed to be similar in difficulty to an official MET and to give you a reasonable idea of what scores you can expect to receive. However, there is no guarantee that your scores and CEFR levels on the practice test will be the same as those you receive when you take the MET.

Section I: Listening

- **Scores 44 and above:** If you have strictly followed the instructions for taking the practice test, you are likely to receive a scaled score that corresponds to CEFR level C1.

- **Scores 32–43:** You are likely to receive a scaled score that corresponds to CEFR level B2.

- **Scores 17–31:** You are likely to receive a scaled score that corresponds to CEFR level B1.

- **Scores 11–16:** You are likely to receive a scaled score that corresponds to CEFR level A2.

- **Scores 10 or below:** You are likely to receive a scaled score below A2 on the CEFR . You may benefit from more lessons or more practice before you register for the examination.

Section II: Reading and Grammar

- **Scores 45 and above:** If you have strictly followed the instructions for taking the practice test, you are likely to receive a scaled score that corresponds to CEFR level C1.

- **Scores 37–44:** You are likely to receive a scaled score that corresponds to CEFR level B2.

- **Scores 22–36:** You are likely to receive a scaled score that corresponds to CEFR level B1.

- **Scores 15–21:** You are likely to receive a scaled score that corresponds to CEFR level A2.

- **Scores 18 or below:** You are likely to receive a scaled score below A2 on the CEFR. You may benefit from more lessons or more practice before you register for the examination.

Section III: Writing

The writing responses are evaluated according to grammatical accuracy, vocabulary, mechanics, cohesion and organization, and task completion. Grammatical accuracy encompasses the number and kinds of errors and the degree to which these affect the intended meaning. Vocabulary is rated according to appropriateness of word choice and range of sophistication. Mechanics refers to the elements of basic writing such as capitalization, punctuation, and spelling. Cohesion and organization refers to the writer's ability to sequence and connect ideas, using clear transitions and connective devices. Task completion is evaluated according to the writer's ability to answer the question fully with enough relevant detail and stay on topic.

When you are finished with the Writing test, ask a teacher or expert English user to compare your responses to the sample writing responses and commentary included in this book. Each of the sample prompts are rated according to CEFR level, and the commentary should serve as a guideline for teachers who can evaluate the completed practice test writing responses. Keep in mind, however, that the Writing test scores you receive when you take the MET under examination conditions are determined by raters who have been trained and certified according to MLA standards. Therefore, it is not possible to assign an exact score on a practice test. Comparing your writing responses to the sample responses in this book will give you an approximation of your writing level.

The public version of the Writing test rating criteria is available at: https://michiganassessment.org/wp-content/uploads/2014/11/MET-Rating-Scale-Writing.pdf

The MET Speaking Test

The criteria for evaluating the Speaking test include task completion, vocabulary and grammar, and intelligibility. Task completion includes, for example, relevance of the response, quantity of language produced, and the amount of supporting detail. Language resources encompasses primarily the range and appropriateness of vocabulary and grammatical accuracy and complexity. Intelligibility includes pronunciation and delivery features such as fluency, rhythm, and hesitation. All Speaking test responses are recorded and rated by trained evaluators, so scores on practice tests cannot be accurately estimated. Students are encouraged to consult with their teachers, test examiners, or other expert users when evaluating their practice attempts on the Speaking test, and use this unofficial feedback to target specific sub-skills for further practice and improvement on the speaking test.

The public version of the Speaking test rating criteria is available at: https://michiganassessment.org/wp-content/uploads/2014/11/MET-RatingScale-Speaking.pdf

Preparing for Test Day

The sample answer sheet in the back of the book is provided so you know what it looks like before taking the test. The instructions that you will see on the actual test are also included with the sample answer sheet. Before your official test date, read over these general test instructions and make sure you understand the answer sheet so you are able to complete it correctly on the day of the test.

Practice Test 1

Listening Section Instructions

In this section of the test, you will show your ability to understand spoken English. There are three parts in this section of the test, with special directions for each part.

Mark your answers in the book. If you do not know the answer, you may guess. Try to answer as many questions as possible.

Part 1

In this part of the test, you will hear short conversations between two people. After each conversation, you will hear a question about it. Choose the best answer to the question from the choices printed in the book. You should mark A, B, C, or D.

There are 19 questions in Part 1. The conversations and questions on the audio will not be repeated. Please listen carefully. Once the audio starts, it will not stop. There is a 12-second pause after each question to give you time to answer.

Do not turn the page until you are told to do so.

Now turn the page.

Listening

1. What happened to the woman's luggage?
   A. It was placed on a later flight.
   B. It was taken by another passenger.
   C. It was sent to the wrong person.
   D. It was damaged.

2. According to the woman, what might help the man decide?
   A. how much he'll spend on housing
   B. how attractive the university's location is
   C. what the university's buildings look like
   D. what is included in the institutional fees

3. What are the speakers mainly discussing?
   A. an employee who is frequently absent
   B. the low number of visitors to a website
   C. technical problems with a website
   D. difficulty contacting a repair company

4. Why did the man miss class?
   A. He was rehearsing with the choir.
   B. He was writing a speech.
   C. He had to meet with a teacher.
   D. He had to finish his homework.

5. What does the man suggest the woman do?
   A. buy clothes in Portugal
   B. travel to Spain
   C. pack warm clothes
   D. bring her sandals

6. What problem does the man have?
   A. He forgot to register for class.
   B. He forgot to get his advisor's signature.
   C. He forgot to go to the first class.
   D. He forgot to bring the form.

7. What does the man want to do?
   A. find out where to buy the cookies
   B. make the cookies
   C. create a different recipe
   D. cook for the woman

8. How does the woman feel about her trip to Paris?
   A. She was disappointed by the weather.
   B. She is happy to be back at work.
   C. She had a hard time getting around there.
   D. She wishes she were still there.

9. What does the man want to buy?
   A. shaving cream
   B. a bar of soap
   C. shampoo
   D. vitamins

10. What happened to the man's plants?
    A. They were planted too late.
    B. They got too much sun.
    C. They got too much water.
    D. They did not have good soil.

11. How does the woman feel about the man's idea?
    A. supportive
    B. confident
    C. upset
    D. unexcited

12. Why does the student talk to the professor?
    A. to find out what he missed in class
    B. to discuss a misunderstanding between classmates
    C. to get advice about a paper he's writing
    D. to ask a question about the reading

13. Why is the man happy about the new employee?
    A. They are business partners.
    B. They used to study together.
    C. He is very well known in their field.
    D. He is interested in European design.

14. What did the woman want?
    A. a discount
    B. a refund
    C. an exchange
    D. a receipt

15. What can be inferred about the professor?
    A. She returned the paper last week.
    B. She has read the man's paper.
    C. She is going to change the assignment.
    D. She prefers American art.

16. How do the speakers feel about the candidates?
    A. disappointed
    B. concerned
    C. pleased
    D. relieved

17. What does the woman say about her haircut?
    A. It did not cost very much.
    B. It is shorter than she wanted.
    C. It is easy to style.
    D. It was not much of a change.

18. What does the man say about the bike?
    A. It took a long time to make.
    B. It was very expensive.
    C. It is heavier than other bikes.
    D. It is not worth what it cost.

19. What is required of the student who gets the scholarship?
    A. working part-time at the firm
    B. recruiting other students to apply
    C. accepting a job at the firm after graduating
    D. developing a new marketing program

End of Part 1.

This page is blank.

Part 2

In this part of the test, you will hear longer conversations between two people. After each conversation, you will answer some questions about it. Choose the best answer to the question from the choices printed in the book. You should mark A, B, C, or D.

There are 14 questions in Part 2. The conversations and questions on the audio will not be repeated. If you want to, you may take notes in your book as you listen. Please listen carefully. Once the audio starts, it will not stop. There is a 12-second pause after each question to give you time to answer.

Do not turn the page until you are told to do so.

Now turn the page.

20. What are the speakers talking about?
    A. types of fitness memberships
    B. becoming fitness instructors
    C. changing the man's membership plan
    D. how to choose a dance class

21. What is the difference between the Basic Pass and the Unlimited Pass?
    A. The Unlimited Pass is less expensive.
    B. The Unlimited Pass includes classes.
    C. The Unlimited Pass is available to all members.
    D. The Unlimited Pass does not expire.

22. What will the man probably do?
    A. ask about other types of memberships
    B. try the more expensive option
    C. continue to exercise by himself
    D. teach a dance class

23. Why does the woman say:
    A. to explain how she learned to dance
    B. to emphasize the variety of classes available
    C. to indicate how often classes meet
    D. to tell the man which classes she attends

24. Why was the woman looking for the man?
    A. to give him a note
    B. to ask him for some help
    C. to show him her project
    D. to tell him a class is canceled

25. What will the man most likely do?
    A. finish the project for the woman
    B. enter the contest with the woman
    C. help the woman think of ideas
    D. find recycled materials for the woman

26. What does the man mean when he says:
    A. He will help her next time.
    B. He already has too much to do.
    C. He thinks the idea is a waste of time.
    D. He is going to be late to class.

27. What are the speakers mainly discussing?
    A. when the book is to be published
    B. where pictures of the dishes will be taken
    C. what recipes to include in the book
    D. how the book will be illustrated

28. What did the woman think of the new recipes?
    A. They are healthier than older recipes.
    B. Some of them need small adjustments.
    C. They are all ready for the book.
    D. Most of them are easy to follow.

29. Why does the man mention the woman's friend?
    A. He wants her friend to work for them.
    B. Her friend is a famous photographer.
    C. Her friend wants to write a book.
    D. He wants to introduce her friend to someone.

30. What does the woman mean when she says:
    A. She agreed to use drawings.
    B. She would rather use photographs.
    C. She'll see how much the drawings cost.
    D. She's not ready to make a decision.

31. What does the woman say about the course?
    A. It is an upper-level course.
    B. It is required for geography majors.
    C. It is only taken by geography majors.
    D. It is only open to second-year students.

32. How does the woman explain the results of her study?
    A. Geography majors must also take other science courses.
    B. Second-year students are generally better at studying.
    C. Background knowledge is not important in geography.
    D. First-year students usually take more courses.

33. What does the man mean when he says:
    A. He understands what the woman said.
    B. The woman's study is well designed.
    C. He has received the woman's study.
    D. The woman has understood correctly.

End of Part 2.

This page is blank.

Part 3

In this part of the test, you will hear some short talks. After each talk, you will answer some questions about it. Choose the best answer to the question from the choices printed in the book. You should mark A, B, C, or D.

There are 17 questions in Part 3. The talks and questions on the audio will not be repeated. If you want to, you may take notes in your book as you listen. Please listen carefully. Once the audio starts, it will not stop. There is a 12-second pause after each question to give you time to answer.

Do not turn the page until you are told to do so.

Now turn the page.

34. Why does the speaker mention creating jobs and reducing pollution?
    A. to discuss a government proposal
    B. to describe the benefits of a project
    C. to give examples of the city's new goals
    D. to explain why people live in the city

35. Why does the speaker thank the local residents?
    A. for driving their cars less
    B. for being patient
    C. for providing suggestions
    D. for giving money to the city

36. Why does the speaker suggest looking at the website?
    A. to look up the train schedule
    B. to find out where Logan Street is
    C. to get information about traffic delays
    D. to read more about the city's history

37. What does the speaker mean when she says: 🔊
    A. The project had to be changed many times.
    B. The project had to be started over.
    C. The project had no public support.
    D. The project had unexpected problems.

38. How does the speaker think the new employees will feel?
    A. relaxed
    B. annoyed
    C. confused
    D. excited

39. What does the speaker want some staff to do?
    A. give a new employee a tour of the building
    B. take a new employee to lunch
    C. meet a new employee at the Human Resources office
    D. help a new employee fill out paperwork

40. What will the staff probably do next?
    A. go back to work
    B. have some coffee
    C. leave for the airport
    D. greet the new employees

41. What does the speaker say about the tech staff?
    A. They'll be assigned new workstations.
    B. They'll fix the online timesheets.
    C. They'll explain the computer system.
    D. They'll send an email message.

42. What is the professor mainly discussing?

    A. how to select instruments for a concert

    B. how to compose concert music

    C. how to choose music for a concert

    D. how to pick a concert to attend

43. Why does the professor mention trumpet players?

    A. to compare them to other musicians

    B. to explain why slow songs are better

    C. to describe a problem he had

    D. to show the type of music audiences prefer

44. What advice is given about challenging music?

    A. Only advanced students should perform it.

    B. It should not be included in a concert.

    C. Players only need five minutes of practice time.

    D. Musicians should practice it on their own.

45. What will the students do next?

    A. describe their favorite band concert

    B. choose which instrument they'd like to play

    C. work on a group project

    D. discuss last week's lecture

46. What does the professor mean when he says:

    A. Playing different styles will keep people interested.

    B. Certain music styles should be avoided.

    C. Playing several styles will confuse people.

    D. Musicians usually request a specific music style.

47. What is the main point of Jerry Hampton's book?

    A. Everyone can run a marathon.

    B. Running shoes are not good for runners.

    C. Running barefoot is dangerous.

    D. Runners need to see their doctors more often.

48. What does Jerry Hampton have in common with other runners?

    A. He was inspired to run by the Tarahumara.

    B. He has gotten injured while running.

    C. He thinks more expensive shoes are safer.

    D. He started running without talking to a doctor.

49. What does the woman think will happen in the future?

    A. More Tarahumara will run in marathons.

    B. More regulations will be created for marathons.

    C. Researchers will test Hampton's theory.

    D. Runners will continue to use expensive shoes.

50. What does the speaker mean when she says:

    A. Hampton no longer agrees with his own theory.

    B. Hampton is not a qualified doctor.

    C. Hampton is a better runner than most doctors.

    D. Hampton will write a book about sports medicine.

End of the Listening test.

This page is blank.

Reading and Grammar Section Instructions

This section of the test focuses on your ability to use English grammar and to understand written English. There are 50 questions in this part of the test. They are numbered 51 to 100.

You will have 65 minutes to complete the entire section. Try to answer all questions. You may answer the questions in any order you wish.

Each question has only one correct answer. Choose the best answer to the question from the choices printed in the book. You should mark A, B, C, or D. If you are not sure about an answer, you may guess.

You may begin now.

GRAMMAR

51. The line _____ for the new art exhibition stretched over two city blocks.
    A. of buying tickets
    B. that tickets are bought
    C. for tickets were bought
    D. to buy tickets

52. The author's new book is _____ her previous one.
    A. more interested that
    B. so interesting than
    C. more interesting than
    D. as much interested

53. They decided to go shopping later because it _____ too hard right now.
    A. has been raining
    B. is raining
    C. will rain
    D. rains

54. The company replaces employee photo ID cards _____ five years.
    A. of each
    B. any
    C. every
    D. all of

55. Chess has been a popular game _____ centuries.
    A. until
    B. for
    C. since
    D. by

56. Professor Kline is wondering _____ best way to maintain discipline in class.
    A. how it could be
    B. what should have been a
    C. what would be the
    D. how it will be

57. _____ size of seats on airplanes will lead to greater comfort for passengers.
    A. By increased the
    B. If increasing in
    C. To increase in
    D. Increasing the

58. To demonstrate proper breathing techniques, my voice instructor _____ for fifteen minutes non-stop.
    A. was used to sing
    B. used to singing
    C. sung
    D. sang

59. Effective presentations are brief and focused _____ time for questions at the end.
    A. that are also allowing
    B. and also allow
    C. yet have also been allowed
    D. so also allows

60. The flowers would have survived the winter if they _____ from the cold.
    A. are protecting
    B. had been protected
    C. protected
    D. had been protecting

61. The children _____ put on their coats and boots.
    A. helped each other
    B. helped one and the other
    C. were helped each
    D. were helped each other

62. Employees who _____ time off in January must notify their supervisor by December 1.
    A. will take their wish
    B. will be wishing they take
    C. wish to be taken
    D. wish to take

63. It would have been nice _____ with him, but I couldn't afford it.
    A. to have traveled
    B. had to travel
    C. have to travel
    D. had traveled

64. Never before _____ so deeply affected by snowfall.
    A. the state's tourism had
    B. the state's tourism is
    C. has the state's tourism been
    D. would be the state's tourism

65. It was not _____ university that he decided to become a biologist.
    A. up to Steve starting
    B. before Steve starts
    C. when Steve has started
    D. until Steve started

66. Our magazine sent one journalist, _____ two photographers, to cover the fashion show.
    A. and together
    B. along with
    C. as well
    D. to start from

67. If the university raises its tuition fees, it _____ a drop in enrollment.
    A. would have been experiencing
    B. will have experienced
    C. would be experiencing
    D. will experience

68. Philip _____ the bus to work; he just walks to the office from home.
    A. hardly ever takes
    B. usually took
    C. occasionally has taken
    D. is always taking

69. _____ change our research topic, we may not find enough reliable sources.
    A. Rather than we
    B. Whether we
    C. Unless we
    D. If we will

70. _____ your old computer is still working, you shouldn't buy a new one.
    A. In order that
    B. Although
    C. As long as
    D. In spite of

Reading and Grammar

READING

This passage is about birth order.

Parenting books and self-help literature typically associate one's birth order with certain personality characteristics. Popular opinion holds that birth order can actually account for these attributes and can give clues about the kind of adult a child might become.

The influence of birth order was first described by psychiatrist Alfred Adler, an associate of Sigmund Freud's and the founder of individual psychology. Adler's writings, published in the early 1900s, were supported by research performed throughout the twentieth century. Studies assigned children roles based on their birth order: first-born children were leaders, rule-followers, and high-achievers. Youngest children were characterized as charming, yet they were thought of as rebels with an independent streak. Those in the middle had good social skills and acted as peacekeepers in their families. Additionally, researchers made attempts to tie birth order to other characteristics like health, career choices, illegal behavior, and even intelligence.

While these personality descriptions agree with popular attitudes toward birth order, scientific research has been mostly unable to consistently reproduce the results of studies analyzing the role of birth order in life outcomes. In part, this is due to the large number of variables that must be taken into account. The number of children in a family, the number of years that separate them, and their genders are a few of the factors that make studying birth order difficult. Researchers also consider a person's "psychological" birth order. Should a child with two siblings, one fifteen years older and one just two years younger, be considered first-born or a middle child? What about twins or triplets? And how should psychologists interpret the effects of step-siblings and half-siblings?

While researchers have not found definitive answers to the birth order debate, one area of study presents an interesting perspective on it. Some research indicates that if a person believes ideas about stereotypical birth order effects on career success, he or she may have career outcomes that match those stereotypes.

71. What does the author mention about Sigmund Freud?
    A. He reviewed his peers' research on birth order.
    B. He inspired a field of research focusing on birth order.
    C. His participation in early birth order studies was important.
    D. His colleague first studied birth order.

72. In the fourth sentence of paragraph 2, what is meant by **rebels**?
    A. people who don't like to follow rules
    B. people who don't form strong relationships
    C. people who are high achieving
    D. people with good social skills

73. Why does the author end paragraph 3 with a series of questions?
    A. to criticize new research in the field
    B. to suggest new lines of research that should be considered
    C. to list variables that affect how birth order is considered
    D. to mention issues the writer is investigating

74. In the first sentence of paragraph 4, what does **it** refer to?
    A. the plan to analyze existing birth order research
    B. the debate about the influence of birth order
    C. a newly completed study about birth order
    D. a theory that rejects the importance of birth order

75. What is the main focus of the research mentioned in the last paragraph?
    A. how birth order stereotypes influence professional results
    B. how families with children of only one gender are affected
    C. the lack of birth order research on families with twins
    D. birth order analysis of families that include step-siblings

This passage is about a species of rat.

Most living organisms have some way of protecting themselves from natural predators. Some mammals, like the platypus, carry internal toxins to transmit to predators via biting or other means, and some plants protect themselves by being poisonous. The African crested rat was originally thought to be poisonous because predators that tried to eat it often became paralyzed. But scientists have recently learned that's not actually the case.

The crested rat chews on the poisonous bark of a certain tree and then smears the chewed-up substance onto its fur, where a strip of special quill-like hairs soaks up the poisonous mixture. Though similar to a porcupine's, the quills do differ: whereas the porcupine defends itself by poking predators, the African rat uses its quill-like hairs to deliver poison to them. When a predator comes after it, instead of running away, the rat stays put and parts its hair to reveal the strip of fur on its back where the poison is being stored. The raised strip is the first thing that receives a bite, and the poison inside disables the predator. These hair tubes are unusual. In fact, scientists do not know of another animal that uses plant poison in this way.

Scientists are puzzled that the rat doesn't appear to be affected by the poison. Because it affects heartbeat regulation, understanding how the rat can keep its heart rate regulated effectively while using the poison could help scientists develop new medicines for people with heart trouble.

76. What is the main purpose of the passage?
    A. to show how animals can affect plant life
    B. to compare one animal to other similar ones
    C. to emphasize the dangers of researching animals
    D. to discuss an unusual animal defense technique

77. In the first paragraph, why does the author mention the platypus?
    A. to illustrate that mammals may eat poisonous plants
    B. to give an example of a mammal that uses poison
    C. to show how it differs from the crested rat
    D. to explain that the platypus is at risk

78. Why does the crested rat chew on tree bark?
    A. to aid in its digestion
    B. to create a poisonous paste
    C. to clean its teeth and fur
    D. to deposit poison on the tree

79. What does the author say a crested rat has in common with a porcupine?
    A. their natural environment
    B. a certain behavior
    C. their regular diet
    D. a physical feature

80. What would scientists like to investigate further?
    A. medicine used to counteract poison
    B. other animals like the crested rat
    C. health effects of a chemical
    D. rats with unhealthy hearts

A

Music News

The John Hamilton Quintet kicks off its three-month world tour at the Jazz Theater on Friday, March 3, at 7:00 p.m. General Admission tickets are $21. They are available at the box office. Students and seniors pay $16.

The John Hamilton Quintet features John Hamilton on guitar, Roy Velasquez on keyboards, Dave Miller on saxophone, Bill Duke on bass, and Mark Richards on drums. The group is promoting its latest album, *Impressions*. During their tour, the group will visit ten countries on four continents.

For more information, go to www.JHQLive.biz or call 555-1212.

B

Critic's Corner

The John Hamilton Quintet performed for a full house at the Jazz Theater on Friday. The audience was treated to an entertaining show led by guitarist John Hamilton.

Intricate ensemble playing and passionate soloing are the group's hallmarks. The band's superb technical abilities and subtle artistry were on full display all night long. The twenty-one-year-old Roy Velasquez turned in an especially remarkable performance. His outstanding solos and spirited support showed maturity uncharacteristic of such a young player. We can look forward to more good things from this rising star.

Mr. Velasquez replaced longtime band member Frank Holmes on keyboards in 2007. The band closed the show with "Holmes Sweet Holmes," a fast-paced tune written by Mr. Velasquez as a tribute to Mr. Holmes, his close friend and mentor.

The John Hamilton Quintet is currently on a three-month world tour, celebrating the release of their latest CD, *Impressions*.

C

Jazz Stories

Award-winning guitarist and accomplished songwriter John Hamilton is fast becoming an institution in American music. The release of *Impressions*, the tenth album made by the John Hamilton Quintet, cements his reputation as a hardworking and prolific musician and a talented bandleader.

Mr. Hamilton was born and raised in Brooklyn, New York. A guitar given to him on his tenth birthday launched the young Hamilton's lifelong creative journey. In high school, he joined the jazz band, where he met Frank Holmes, who at age fourteen was already recognized as a piano virtuoso. The two quickly formed a close and enduring friendship and would go on to play together in several professional bands and collaborate on various musical projects.

Shortly after graduating from the New York College of Music, where he studied composition and arrangement, Mr. Hamilton formed his first band, the John Hamilton Trio. The trio included Mr. Holmes on keyboards and Mark Richards on drums, who had roomed together in college. These three men forged a long-lasting musical partnership, culminating in the John Hamilton Quintet.

The JHQ, as it is known to its scores of fans, has undergone several transformations. The first three albums were recorded with the founding trio plus a saxophonist and a bassist. Although the sax and bass players were replaced over the years, Mr. Holmes did not retire until 2007. He was replaced by the young prodigy Roy Velasquez.

The current lineup consists of Hamilton, Velasquez, and Richards, accompanied by Dave Miller on saxophone and Bill Duke on bass. Together the quintet has recorded three award-winning albums. Critics believe that the widely acclaimed *Impressions* may be the next in line for such recognition.

Refer to page 30 when answering the questions below.

The following questions refer to section A.

81. How can people buy tickets to see the band?
    A. on the website
    B. at the theater
    C. by telephone
    D. from the band

82. Why is the band traveling around the world?
    A. to play with other famous musicians
    B. to get inspiration for new music
    C. to record their live performances
    D. to sell their new music

The following questions refer to section B.

83. What is the main purpose of the article?
    A. to advertise a concert
    B. to describe a musician
    C. to review a performance
    D. to discuss a CD

84. In the last sentence of paragraph 2, what does **this rising star** refer to?
    A. a solo
    B. a musician
    C. the band
    D. the performance

85. Why did the band play "Holmes Sweet Holmes"?
    A. because it is a new song
    B. because the song is so famous
    C. out of respect for a former member
    D. to replace a song written by Holmes

The following questions refer to section C.

86. How did John Hamilton become interested in music?
    A. He met Frank Holmes.
    B. He attended a performance as a child.
    C. He received an instrument as a gift.
    D. He heard *Impressions*.

87. What does the author suggest about Frank Holmes?
    A. He is still playing live music.
    B. His first instrument was guitar.
    C. His talent was obvious from a young age.
    D. He first began to study piano in college.

88. Why does the author mention JHQ?
    A. It is the name of an award-winning album.
    B. It is what the public calls the band.
    C. It is the band's new name.
    D. It is what people call John Hamilton.

89. In the second sentence of paragraph 4, which word is closest in meaning to **founding**?
    A. primary
    B. popular
    C. young
    D. original

The following question refers to two or more sections.

90. What is mentioned in all three passages?
    A. Roy Velasquez's solo ability
    B. Frank Holmes's retirement
    C. the band's tour schedule
    D. the band's current album

A

Volunteers Wanted

Join us for archaeology fieldwork at the Dorwood Island dig. Volunteers will help transport equipment and supplies, remove soil, and catalog findings.

Dates: May 18 – June 14

Space is limited – sign up soon! Ability to stay at least two weeks is essential, and preference will be given to those who can stay the entire month.

Participants will be provided with food, lodging, archaeological training and equipment, and ground transportation from Simon Airport on Dorwood Island to the dig site. Airfare to Simon Airport not included.

Contact: Dr. Roberta Castillo, rcastillo@blakelee.edu

B

A Month on Dorwood Island

by Rose Johnson

Participating in the Dorwood dig was an exceptional experience, one that reaffirmed my decision to earn my bachelor's degree in cultural anthropology. In fact, I am now considering doing an advanced degree in the field.

It's hard to describe the feeling I had my first morning on the site when I examined the recently discovered rock art. Looking at paintings that might be a thousand years old was captivating. Questions surged through my mind: Who created this art? Why did they create it? When did they create it? I can now see that the answers to these questions will not only provide information about a specific site but will also add to the pool of knowledge about all of humanity's ancestors.

On a practical level, I learned numerous techniques from Dr. Castillo for uncovering, protecting, and analyzing artifacts that I am sure will benefit me on future digs. And on a personal level, Dorwood Island was a beautiful and fun place to spend four weeks; I became friends with many of the people who were helping me to learn so much.

C

Rock Art on Dorwood Island

Dr. Roberta Castillo, professor of archaeology at Blakelee University and director of Culture Connect, a group that links volunteer workers with archaeological projects, recently reported the discovery of a large quantity of petroglyphs—or rock art—in a previously unknown cave on Dorwood Island. The cave was found by a local farmer who was clearing trees.

There are twelve panels of the art in the cave's main chamber displaying designs drawn with charcoal or ochre. The ochre, which is a pigment made from a reddish-yellow mineral oxide, and charcoal were mixed with a binding agent such as blood or egg so that they would adhere to the cave walls.

Most of the drawings in the cave are abstract, such as a circle with a dot in the center, or parallel wavy lines. There is a particularly detailed drawing of a basket, as well as a few handprints. The cave also has natural formations made of mineral deposits, known as stalagmites. Several of the stalagmites had been modified to create artistic figures or designs.

Dr. Castillo, an expert in rock art dating, will use carbon-14 testing and chemical residue analysis to establish the age of the artifacts in the cave. To determine the age of the ochre drawings, a recently developed method that tests for organic binders will be employed. Tests on excavated samples of pottery, animal bones, and charcoal from the cave will be conducted concurrently for cross-dating purposes. It is hoped that the paintings and carvings in the cave will help researchers determine the identity of the people who inhabited the island, as well as shed light on their ritual practices.

Refer to page 32 when answering the questions below.

The following questions refer to section A.

91. What is the purpose of the passage?
    A. to explain what volunteers should bring with them
    B. to inform people about an opportunity to volunteer
    C. to inform volunteers of the deadline for paying fees
    D. to explain the goal of a project to potential volunteers

92. What is required of volunteers?
    A. willingness to spend two weeks on the island
    B. enrolling in Dr. Castillo's course
    C. contributing financially to the project
    D. previous archaeological experience

The following questions refer to section B.

93. Why did the author write this passage?
    A. to provide information about analyzing artifacts
    B. to encourage people to visit Dorwood Island
    C. to convince Dr. Castillo to lead a dig
    D. to report on her experience on a dig

94. How did working on the dig affect the author?
    A. She will change her major to cultural anthropology.
    B. She will apply for a job to work with Dr. Castillo.
    C. She wants to continue studying cultural anthropology.
    D. She wants to write about the art on Dorwood Island.

95. What did the author learn?
    A. how to create rock art
    B. why Dr. Castillo became an archaeologist
    C. the history of the people on Dorwood Island
    D. methods for studying artifacts

The following questions refer to section C.

96. What does Culture Connect do?
    A. assigns workers to projects
    B. promotes the art of native cultural groups
    C. obtains funding for excavation projects
    D. preserves cultures that are in danger of disappearing

97. Why does the author mention egg?
    A. to describe the shapes of some images
    B. to explain how ochre gets its yellow color
    C. to explain how pigments stuck to walls
    D. to describe the ancient artists' diet

98. In the third sentence of paragraph 4, what does the word **concurrently** mean?
    A. at the same time
    B. using a similar process
    C. with extreme care
    D. at a different location

99. What does the author imply about the creators of the art?
    A. Scientists do not believe they lived on the island.
    B. They did not engage in ritual practices.
    C. They did not value abstract images.
    D. Scientists do not know who they were.

The following question refers to two or more sections.

100. What is probably true about Dr. Castillo?
    A. She thinks the art on Dorwood Island is fake.
    B. She discovered the rock art on Dorwood Island.
    C. She has not yet been to Dorwood Island.
    D. She is supervising the Dorwood Island dig.

End of the Reading and Grammar test.

Writing Test Instructions

This writing test has two parts:

- You have 45 minutes to complete both parts.
- Your responses to both parts should be written in this book.
- You will not be graded on the appearance of your paper, but your handwriting must be readable. You may change or correct your writing, but you should not recopy your entire response.

1. When the examiner tells you to, begin Task 1.
2. When you are done with Task 1, continue on to Task 2.

Do not begin until the examiner tells you to.

Task 1

● **Write sentences to answer the questions.**

1. Do you like meeting people? How often do you meet new people?

_____

_____

_____

2. Where is a good place to meet new people?

_____

_____

_____

3. Tell us about an interesting person that you met.

_____

_____

_____

Writing

- **Write paragraphs to answer the question.**
- **Write about 1 to 2 pages. Your test will be marked down if it is extremely short.**

Some people believe workers should have to retire, or stop working, at a certain age. Other people believe that older people's experiences can help a company. Do you think there should be a required retirement age? Explain, giving specific reasons for your choice.

_____

_____

_____

_____

_____

_____

_____

_____

_____

_____

_____

_____

_____

This page is blank.

PRACTICE TEST 2

Listening Section Instructions

In this section of the test, you will show your ability to understand spoken English. There are three parts in this section of the test, with special directions for each part.

Mark your answers in the book. If you do not know the answer, you may guess. Try to answer as many questions as possible.

Part 1

In this part of the test, you will hear short conversations between two people. After each conversation, you will hear a question about it. Choose the best answer to the question from the choices printed in the book. You should mark A, B, C, or D.

There are 19 questions in Part 1. The conversations and questions on the audio will not be repeated. Please listen carefully. Once the audio starts, it will not stop. There is a 12-second pause after each question to give you time to answer.

Do not turn the page until you are told to do so.

Now turn the page.

1. What does the woman want to do?
   A. try on a different shirt
   B. ask for the man's opinion
   C. buy a shirt in a different color
   D. find clothes that are on sale

2. Why is the man disappointed?
   A. He thinks the conference is disorganized.
   B. He had to cancel his speech.
   C. He isn't interested in the workshops.
   D. He couldn't attend the welcome dinner.

3. What will the man do in the summer?
   A. graduate
   B. take classes
   C. go on vacation
   D. work

4. Why did the man repeat the woman's question?
   A. He thought she had gotten his order wrong.
   B. He did not expect the question.
   C. He did not hear the question.
   D. He wanted to make sure she understood him.

5. Why will the woman go to corporate headquarters?
   A. She has to attend an important meeting.
   B. She needs to make an urgent delivery.
   C. She has to sign for a package.
   D. She gave the courier the wrong package.

6. What problem does the man have?
   A. His job is interfering with his studies.
   B. He can't decide which classes to take.
   C. He has too many classes this term.
   D. His assignments are too difficult.

7. What is true about the woman's new car?
   A. It uses less gas than her old car.
   B. It is larger than her old car.
   C. It costs more to drive.
   D. It is the fastest car on the market.

8. What will the woman do next?
   A. read a journal article
   B. grade her students' work
   C. make a list of things to do
   D. take a break

9. How do the bookcases compare?
   A. The pine bookcases are less expensive.
   B. The pine bookcases are smaller.
   C. The oak bookcases are more popular.
   D. The oak bookcases look better.

10. What happened to the woman?
    A. She didn't complete her assignment properly.
    B. Her professor did not return her paper.
    C. She didn't know when the assignment was due.
    D. The man helped her with her paper.

11. What does the man say about his job?

   A. He expected more from it.
   B. It was not a wise choice.
   C. He is starting to like it.
   D. It does not pay well.

12. How does the man feel?

   A. He feels distracted.
   B. He likes his new computer.
   C. He actually wanted some luggage.
   D. He feels disappointed.

13. What will the man ask the professor?

   A. what the topic of his presentation should be
   B. who will give the first presentation
   C. how to prepare for the exam
   D. when the exam will be given

14. What does the man think is required for the job?

   A. the ability to work quickly
   B. extensive work experience
   C. a flexible schedule
   D. current technical knowledge

15. What is the woman planning to do?

   A. borrow a map from the man
   B. purchase a guidebook
   C. take a vacation
   D. go on a walk with the man

16. What will the presentation be on?

   A. technical improvements in security
   B. new forms of human relationships
   C. new designs to use on internet sites
   D. common problems with human interaction

17. What will probably happen next?

   A. The woman will check the man's account balance.
   B. The man will speak with another bank employee.
   C. The man will begin working at a new job.
   D. The woman will bring the man some documents.

18. What will the woman do next?

   A. call the student who needs a tutor
   B. schedule a time to meet again
   C. talk to someone else about the job
   D. give the man some more information

19. What does the man need to do?

   A. call his brother and ask for help
   B. tell his landlord about the broken pipe
   C. live somewhere else for a while
   D. stay home to clean up his apartment

End of Part 1.

This page is blank.

Part 2

In this part of the test, you will hear longer conversations between two people. After each conversation, you will answer some questions about it. Choose the best answer to the question from the choices printed in the book. You should mark A, B, C, or D.

There are 14 questions in Part 2. The conversations and questions on the audio will not be repeated. If you want to, you may take notes in your book as you listen. Please listen carefully. Once the audio starts, it will not stop. There is a 12-second pause after each question to give you time to answer.

Do not turn the page until you are told to do so.

Now turn the page.

20. What is the store's problem?
    A. The manager is unavailable to answer questions.
    B. The customers are confused about a sales display.
    C. The store doesn't sell formal shoes.
    D. The staff doesn't know which shoes are discounted.

21. Which shoes are on sale?
    A. the shoes under the sign
    B. only the black shoes
    C. all the shoes on the table
    D. all the formal shoes

22. What did the woman offer to ask the manager?
    A. whether other formal shoes are available
    B. when the formal shoes go on sale
    C. whether she can offer a special price
    D. when the customer can talk to him

23. What does the woman mean when she says:
    A. The shoes are more formal.
    B. The shoes are more affordable.
    C. The shoes are more comfortable.
    D. The shoes are more attractive.

24. Why does the man visit the office?
    A. to sign up for a university social event
    B. to register for classes for next semester
    C. to inquire about a job opportunity
    D. to ask for directions to the student union

25. How does the man feel about his time at the university?
    A. He's frustrated with his new living situation.
    B. He's enjoying himself but wants to meet people.
    C. He's relieved that the classes aren't too difficult.
    D. He's bored and wants to find a job.

26. What does the woman mean when she says:
    A. Everyone will be given food and drink.
    B. Everyone will have to register at the event.
    C. The organizers will teach people new information.
    D. The organizers will help people feel comfortable.

27. What are the speakers mainly talking about?

    A. driving in the area

    B. the street construction

    C. the woman's work schedule

    D. a new coffee shop

28. Why is the man upset?

    A. The construction workers don't buy coffee.

    B. Work near his shop is taking longer than planned.

    C. Customers may not come to his shop.

    D. The street will be closed to traffic.

29. What is probably true about the woman's coffee drinking?

    A. She regularly buys coffee at the man's shop.

    B. She is trying to drink less coffee.

    C. She doesn't use cream in her coffee.

    D. She doesn't drink coffee every day.

30. What does the man mean when he says:

    A. He wants to know what the woman thinks.

    B. He thinks it will not affect his business.

    C. He wants to know the woman's plans.

    D. He thinks nothing can be done about it.

31. What problem does the student have?

    A. He didn't understand the reading assignment.

    B. He cannot afford to go to the play.

    C. He doesn't have time to read the play.

    D. He has to work on Saturday.

32. Why did the professor wait to buy the tickets?

    A. She had forgotten to buy them sooner.

    B. She wanted a reduced price.

    C. She didn't know how many students would attend.

    D. She had problems finding the theater.

33. Why did the student interrupt the professor?

    A. She was giving him the wrong information.

    B. She was giving him the wrong paper.

    C. She was making an incorrect assumption.

    D. She was causing him to be late for work.

End of Part 2.

This page is blank.

Part 3

In this part of the test, you will hear some short talks. After each talk, you will answer some questions about it. Choose the best answer to the question from the choices printed in the book. You should mark A, B, C, or D.

There are 17 questions in Part 3. The talks and questions on the audio will not be repeated. If you want to, you may take notes in your book as you listen. Please listen carefully. Once the audio starts, it will not stop. There is a 12-second pause after each question to give you time to answer.

Do not turn the page until you are told to do so.

Now turn the page.

34. What is the talk mainly about?
    A. the abilities needed in order to count
    B. the features of counting systems
    C. animals' ability to communicate
    D. ways of grouping objects

35. What will the professor probably discuss in the next lecture?
    A. monkeys' use of symbols to communicate differences
    B. features of advanced counting systems
    C. labeling categories without using words or numbers
    D. the parts of the brain used when comparing

36. What does the professor say about distinguishing small numbers from large numbers?
    A. It isn't as important as being able to count.
    B. It is easy for most animals to do.
    C. It isn't the same as counting.
    D. It is something humans do naturally.

37. What does the professor mean when she says: 🔊
    A. The number of objects is different.
    B. The location of the difference is important.
    C. The difference in amount is important.
    D. The category labels are different.

38. What is the speaker mainly discussing?
    A. how to avoid bicycle theft
    B. how to ride a bicycle safely
    C. how to secure things to a bicycle
    D. how to protect a home from thieves

39. Why does the speaker mention garages?
    A. Most properties should have one.
    B. Many items are stolen from them.
    C. They are less safe than a house.
    D. Bicycles are safer if kept in them.

40. What does the speaker state about locking a bicycle?
    A. never lock the frame to a bike rack
    B. lock it to another bicycle
    C. never lock both wheels
    D. lock it to something solid

41. According to the speaker, what should bike users do in addition to locking their bikes?
    A. use only a modern lock
    B. study where thieves commonly operate
    C. buy a good set of bike lights
    D. be careful with removable items

42. What is the speaker's main purpose?
    A. to describe how calories are added to beverages
    B. to discuss a problem in children's diets
    C. to compare different studies about children's diets
    D. to explain the health benefit of certain beverages

43. What does the study show about children's diet twenty years ago?
    A. Children's daily calorie intake was very low.
    B. Children consumed fewer sugary beverages.
    C. Children got more nutrients from their drinks.
    D. Children got more vitamins from their drinks.

44. Why does the speaker mention "empty calories"?
    A. to indicate sugary drinks have little nutritional value
    B. to suggest they make up most of children's diets
    C. to illustrate different types of food children consume
    D. to discuss features of foods high in sugar

45. What did the study find is true about many teens in the United States?
    A. They drink more sugary beverages when they exercise.
    B. They're getting more calories than necessary from drinks.
    C. They're getting most of their vitamins from beverages.
    D. They prefer sugary beverages to healthier drinks.

46. What does the speaker mean when she says:
    A. The calorie increase is more significant than it seems.
    B. The number of calories is growing fast.
    C. The calorie increase is larger than researchers expected.
    D. The actual number of calories is unknown.

47. Why is the woman speaking to the employees?
    A. to explain a new policy
    B. to discuss a new manager's schedule
    C. to train new employees
    D. to announce changes to a procedure

48. Why does the woman think that employees will approve of the vacation policy?
    A. Employees get all their vacation at one time.
    B. Some employees will earn more vacation than before.
    C. Everyone will earn vacation for the first time.
    D. Fewer employees will take the same days off.

49. What must an employee do in order to take time off?
    A. contact the woman
    B. ask a supervisor in advance
    C. work extra hours another day
    D. find another employee to work that time

50. What does the speaker mean when she says:
    A. The employees will get time off if possible.
    B. Few employees are allowed to take vacation.
    C. The company must refuse most requests.
    D. Many employees forget to request time off.

End of the Listening test.

This page is blank.

Reading and Grammar Section Instructions

This section of the test focuses on your ability to use English grammar and to understand written English. There are 50 questions in this part of the test. They are numbered 51 to 100.

You will have 65 minutes to complete the entire section. Try to answer all questions. You may answer the questions in any order you wish.

Each question has only one correct answer. Choose the best answer to the question from the choices printed in the book. You should mark A, B, C, or D. If you are not sure about an answer, you may guess.

You may begin now.

Reading and Grammar

GRAMMAR

51. Jane _____ part-time at the supermarket until she graduates this summer.
    - A. has worked
    - B. worked
    - C. is working
    - D. was working

52. On public holidays, the university's science library _____ open until noon.
    - A. aren't
    - B. hasn't
    - C. weren't
    - D. doesn't

53. When I talked to my sister on the phone, I told _____.
    - A. to her your new job
    - B. your new job for her
    - C. of your new job her
    - D. her about your new job

54. She had scrambled eggs and _____ toast for breakfast this morning.
    - A. never as much
    - B. a couple of slices of
    - C. not too many
    - D. a small number of

55. John's chemistry teacher inspired _____ college.
    - A. to him to applying
    - B. that he applied to
    - C. for his applying
    - D. him to apply to

56. This latest report is _____ the previous one.
    - A. considerably more detailed than
    - B. of a more considerable detail
    - C. more considerable in detail to
    - D. in considerably more detailed

57. _____ the next intersection, and the bookstore will be on your right.
    - A. Turn left at
    - B. To turn left on
    - C. Turn around left
    - D. Turning left into

58. The conflict among the players _____ the team comes to a consensus.
    - A. will not be resolved unless
    - B. has been resolved except
    - C. will not resolve without
    - D. to be resolved only if

59. Campus police officers remove bicycles parked _____ other than the designated bike racks.
    - A. out of
    - B. wherever
    - C. anywhere
    - D. away from

60. I have been training for weeks _____ I'll be ready to run the marathon.
    - A. even if
    - B. so that
    - C. as long as
    - D. in order for

61. I _____ to bring my keys before leaving the dormitory.
    A. should have thought
    B. can think
    C. should be thinking
    D. will have thought

62. The new law requires all motorcyclists _____ helmets.
    A. to wear
    B. who wear their
    C. that must wear
    D. for wearing

63. This is the last reminder for any student _____ to submit a scholarship application.
    A. hasn't yet applied
    B. who hasn't yet applied
    C. whoever is applying
    D. that he applies

64. _____ from medicine in 2004, Dr. Porter became a writer of short stories and poems.
    A. When retirement
    B. Since retired
    C. Before he retires
    D. After retiring

65. If I _____ far behind schedule myself, I'd help you with your history project.
    A. hadn't been much
    B. haven't been more
    C. wasn't such a
    D. weren't so

66. I thought _____ paid for Fran's conference expenses last week.
    A. that were it the company
    B. it was the company that
    C. the company that was
    D. that were the company

67. Under no circumstances _____ taken from the laboratory.
    A. test equipment had been
    B. test equipment would have
    C. should test equipment be
    D. could be that test equipment

68. _____ the change of seasons, I prefer to live where it's warm.
    A. Even though I enjoy
    B. Yet to enjoy
    C. Since I have enjoyed
    D. However I am enjoying

69. We need to decide how _____ conduct the new customer service training program.
    A. often to
    B. much longer
    C. seldom for
    D. many to

70. It would have been unthinkable _____ university without a computer.
    A. to have been gone
    B. going to be at
    C. to have gone to
    D. going to go

READING

This passage is about coins.

Coins give historians valuable insight into the lives of ancient people. The images and inscriptions they carry tell about the political and economic aspects of the societies. We can also learn about technological development and trading practices by studying where the metal came from and how the coins were minted.

Tools, such as x-ray fluorescence, can determine the composition of the exterior of ancient coins without altering them. In order to analyze the interior with only minimal damage, researchers drill into the edges. The tiny samples, or turnings, extracted from the interior are analyzed by sophisticated techniques that identify the presence, and even the source, of various metals. For example, the isotopes of lead in the metal produce a chemical "fingerprint." By comparing the value of the isotopes in the coin with that of different silver mines, we learn that the metal in some coins from the early Roman Empire did not come from Italy but from Spain, Britain, and India.

Analyses reveal that prior to about 50 BCE, Roman coins were 99 percent pure silver. A small amount of copper was often added to make the silver harder. Beginning with the emperor Nero, the heart metal of the coins contained a large percentage of copper, which let the emperors mint many coins from a small amount of silver. By compromising the quality of the coins, they solved the financial problems that resulted from heavy spending on military exploits and big building projects. However, the added copper gave the coins an obvious pink color. In order to conceal the loss of value of the currency from the public, the emperors practiced depletion silvering. This technique used acid to dissolve some of the copper from the surface, leaving only the silver. It gave the impression that the coins were pure throughout.

71. What is the main topic of the passage?
    A. the economic development of ancient societies
    B. the technology of the manufacturing of ancient coins
    C. ancient coins as a source of historical information
    D. origins of the use of currency in ancient societies

72. In the second sentence of paragraph 1, what does the word **they** refer to?
    A. coins
    B. people
    C. historians
    D. inscriptions

73. What was learned from studying isotopes of lead in Roman coins?
    A. The origin of the metal could be identified.
    B. The minting technology was highly developed.
    C. Poor quality silver was used in the empire's early years.
    D. The coins were made by melting down foreign coins.

74. Why did Roman emperors change the composition of the coins?
    A. to make the coins easier to inscribe
    B. to make the coins more attractive
    C. to improve the economy
    D. to deceive their enemies

75. In the sixth sentence of paragraph 3, what does the word **depletion** mean?
    A. reinforcement
    B. covering
    C. falsifying
    D. removal

This passage is about a music festival.

Every year, jazz lovers from around the world journey to a small city in California to attend the Monterey Jazz Festival, one of the oldest outdoor music festivals in the United States. This annual three-day event has featured some of the greatest jazz artists of all time.

The festival was founded by San Francisco jazz radio broadcaster Jimmy Lyons and journalist Ralph Gleason. Their goal was to offer a West Coast alternative to the Newport Jazz Festival. As part of their mission to gain the support of local business leaders and city officials, the founders exposed these people to jazz music and artists. For example, they invited famed jazz pianist Dave Brubeck to meet them and give a private performance.

The first festival took place in 1958. Originally only intended as a jazz venue, the festival began to include blues, gospel, some rock, and even world music in the 1960s. Over the years, other types of events occurred there, such as Louis Armstrong's only live stage performance of the musical *The Real Ambassadors* in 1962. The musical is a fictionalized story related to Armstrong's tours around the world as cultural ambassador for the U.S. State Department. In 1970, actor and director Clint Eastwood filmed scenes of the festival to include in his directorial debut, the thriller *Play Misty for Me*.

Now more than five hundred jazz artists perform annually on nine stages throughout the Monterey Fairgrounds. Attendees can also participate in panel discussions, jazz clinics, and workshops. These activities are related to the festival's mission, which is to continue the tradition of this unique musical genre. For this reason, it also donates its annual proceeds to jazz education programs and provides scholarships to musicians and vocalists to attend the prestigious Berklee College of Music in Boston.

76. What can be inferred about the Newport Jazz Festival?
    A. It was replaced by the Monterey Jazz Festival.
    B. It is older than the Monterey Jazz Festival.
    C. It is sometimes held in California.
    D. It was started by Lyons and Gleason.

77. Why did Lyons and Gleason invite Dave Brubeck to Monterey?
    A. to ask him to play at a festival's opening
    B. to help them choose a festival location
    C. to interview him about playing at festivals
    D. to help win approval for a festival

78. How did the Monterey Jazz Festival change in the 1960s?
    A. It gained more community support.
    B. It was held in locations worldwide.
    C. It featured more types of music.
    D. It began to show musical films.

79. What was special about Louis Armstrong's appearance at the festival in 1962?
    A. He was asked to perform world music that year.
    B. His performance appeared in the film *Play Misty for Me*.
    C. He was invited to perform by the U.S. State Department.
    D. He performed in the show *The Real Ambassadors*.

80. What is an important goal of the festival?
    A. to raise money for local businesses
    B. to promote awareness of jazz
    C. to establish a music school
    D. to provide a venue for film directors

A | Field Trip to Hamilton Park

Date: October 10
Meeting Time: 8 a.m. sharp!
Meeting Place: School parking lot

You'll search for and collect animal fossils from over 65 million years ago in the stream at the park.

What you should bring:
- rubber boots
- plastic bags
- a notebook

Hammers and chisels are not necessary. You can easily find fossils by lightly moving the sand on the bottom of the stream. You may keep **no more than five** fossils.

Note: Attendance is required! If you miss this trip, your class grade will be affected.

B | Earth Sciences | Paleontology

Paleontology is the study of ancient life based on fossil evidence. Fossils are the remains or traces of organisms that lived thousands or millions of years ago. *Body fossils*, such as shells, bones, and roots, are the preserved part of the animal or plant after it has died. *Trace fossils*, such as footprints, tracks, and tunnels, are marks left behind by the organism while it was alive.

Paleontologists can quickly locate animal body fossils that are preserved in soft soil, like sand or mud, and collect them by hand. It takes much longer, however, to find fossils located in hard rock. These fossils are only uncovered after erosion—due to wind, rain, and other weather conditions—has worn away the rock. Paleontologists then can spot body or trace fossils and break them loose with tools such as hammers and chisels.

C | Fossil Collecting
The Good, the Bad, and the Ugly

Amateur fossil collectors contribute greatly to the field of paleontology. These nonprofessional collectors routinely make important discoveries when they dig on private and public land where searching for fossils is allowed. In fact, the fossil collections displayed in most museums feature a large number of donations from amateur collectors. While many donate their finds to museums, others choose to keep their fossils or trade them with other collectors, which is a harmless practice provided it's done merely as a hobby and not for financial gain.

Unfortunately, some amateur collectors decide to turn their hobby into a profit-making business and end up becoming commercial fossil collectors. A plant or fish fossil in good condition can sell for hundreds or thousands of dollars, and a dinosaur fossil may be worth millions of dollars.

A few commercial collectors do donate fossils to museums, but the vast majority regrettably choose to sell their fossils to private collectors willing to pay large amounts of money. Most scientists and museums cannot afford to pay high prices for fossils. Once a private collector purchases a fossil, scientists are unable to study it and, therefore, a valuable chance to learn about Earth's past is wasted.

Commercial collectors argue that millions of uncollected fossils are destroyed every year by continued exposure to heavy rain, strong winds, and other weather conditions. They say scientists would not have been able to study them anyway. However, this claim is not valid because it takes a long time for a fossil to be destroyed by weathering. That gives scientists a large window of opportunity to locate and study fossils before they are worn away by the elements. But when fossils are sold to private collectors as soon as they're discovered, that opportunity is lost, possibly forever.

Refer to page 56 when answering the questions below.

The following question refers to section A.

81. What is the purpose of the field trip?
    A. to observe animals
    B. to study how a stream formed
    C. to find fossils
    D. to collect water samples

The following questions refer to section B.

82. In the first paragraph, why does the author mention tunnels?
    A. They are examples of trace fossils.
    B. They are good places to find fossils.
    C. They often contain live organisms.
    D. They usually are older than body fossils.

83. What does the author say about soft soil?
    A. It takes less time to discover fossils in it.
    B. It requires special tools to search for fossils.
    C. It has fewer fossils than hard rock.
    D. It preserves fossils longer than hard rock.

84. In the last sentence of paragraph 2, what does the word **them** refer to?
    A. tools
    B. fossils
    C. paleontologists
    D. rocks

The following questions refer to section C.

85. What is true of most museum fossil collections?
    A. They have fossils discovered by amateurs.
    B. They are often in poor condition.
    C. They tend to be small.
    D. They are funded by commercial collectors.

86. What is the author's opinion about fossil collecting?
    A. It should only be done by professionals.
    B. It is a dangerous hobby.
    C. It should not be done for profit.
    D. It has become too expensive.

87. What is probably true about fossils owned by private collectors?
    A. Museum fossils cost more than they do.
    B. Someone stole them.
    C. Scientists cannot study them.
    D. Scientists are not interested in studying them.

88. What do commercial collectors say about weathering?
    A. It destroys many fossils before scientists can find them.
    B. It helps scientists determine how old fossils are.
    C. It makes collecting fossils easier.
    D. It affects some types of fossils more than others.

The following questions refer to two or more sections.

89. What would the author of section C probably suggest visitors to Hamilton Fossil Park do?
    A. give the fossils they find to a private collector
    B. leave all fossils they find at the park
    C. try to find fossils preserved within rock
    D. donate important fossils they find to a museum

90. How does section B differ from sections A and C?
    A. It compares different types of collectors.
    B. It discusses problems caused by fossil collectors.
    C. It doesn't involve amateur fossil collectors.
    D. It doesn't show how weather affects fossil collecting.

A

We recycle old computer monitors and television sets from:

- Businesses
- Homes
- Schools

Old computer monitors and televisions can be hazardous to the environment. They contain materials that can cause serious health threats if they get into the air or water. Don't let your old monitor or television wind up in a landfill or dump.

FREE Pickup!*

Call Green Tubes at 1-800-RECYCLE!

We'll haul away your old equipment — FREE!*

*Some restrictions apply. Contact us for details.

B

Ask the Doctor

Q: I work on computers all day and have been experiencing intense neck pain. Could improper monitor positioning be the culprit?

A: You should contact a health-care professional to determine the exact cause of your problem. However, you may want to try these two basic tips for proper monitor alignment.

- First, the monitor should be placed directly in front of you at a comfortable distance from your eyes. One good way to determine the right distance is to sit back in your chair and extend your arm. If your monitor is average size, you should be able to touch the screen with the tips of your fingers. However, if your screen is 20 inches or greater, it should be positioned slightly further back.

- Also, your monitor should be raised so that you don't need to tilt your head to see things comfortably. Ideally, your viewing height should be around 2 inches below the top of an 18-inch screen. For larger screens, the top of the viewing area should be 3 or 4 inches above eye level.

I hope this helps!

C

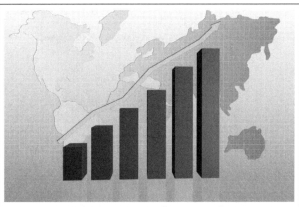

More Computer Screen Space Improves Productivity

The secret to more efficiency in the office may be just a few inches away. A recent study suggests that more computer screen space can significantly improve work productivity.

The study involved office workers of different levels of ability. The first group used standard 18-inch screen monitors. The second group tried two different monitor configurations. One of these configurations was a combination of two 20-inch screen monitors. The second configuration was a single 24-inch widescreen monitor. First, researchers timed both groups as workers did basic editing tasks. Then, they compared the performance of both groups. Results showed that workers using double 20-inch and single 24-inch screen monitors worked about twice as fast as the other workers.

Researchers noticed that double and widescreen monitors performed differently according to task type. The 24-inch widescreen configuration offered the best results for text-editing tasks, such as cutting and pasting. In comparison, the dual 20-inch configuration proved to be the best option for editing information in grids and tables. Workers' level of expertise was also a distinguishing factor. Less-experienced workers benefited the most from using 24-inch widescreen monitors. This suggests that larger monitors can help reduce the productivity gap between novice and experienced office workers.

Two basic reasons account for the results of the study. First, editing jobs usually involve checking multiple pages of text or data at the same time. When more screen space is available, users can view several document pages simultaneously. Because workers in the second group spent less time going back and forth between pages, they were able to work faster than participants in the first group. Finally, workers in the second group reported that the larger screens made editing feel less tiresome. It appears that the increased comfort helped them stay focused for longer periods of time, thus increasing their productivity.

Refer to page 58 when answering the questions below.

The following question refers to section A.

91. In the last line, what does the word **apply** mean?
    A. are requested
    B. are possible
    C. may be affected
    D. have been registered

The following questions refer to section B.

92. What is the main purpose of the passage?
    A. to introduce common causes of work-related accidents
    B. to offer suggestions for positioning a monitor appropriately
    C. to discuss different problems caused by improper monitor use
    D. to describe possible treatments for neck injuries

93. In paragraph 1, what does **culprit** mean?
    A. consequence of a mistake
    B. cause of a problem
    C. cure for a condition
    D. person to blame

94. In the last sentence of the third paragraph, what does **it** refer to?
    A. screen
    B. chair
    C. arm
    D. distance

95. Why should monitors be raised?
    A. to allow users to keep their heads straight
    B. to help users to see smaller images better
    C. to keep the screen away from users' eyes
    D. to allow more than one monitor to be used

The following questions refer to section C.

96. What is the main conclusion of the study?
    A. Computer screen space influences work speed.
    B. Standard 18-inch screen monitors save more energy.
    C. People using larger monitors usually work longer hours.
    D. Experienced editors prefer widescreen monitors.

97. What did results show about workers in Group 1?
    A. They could see things on screen more comfortably.
    B. They produced half as much as Group 2.
    C. They needed more time to understand their tasks.
    D. They completed their tasks before Group 2.

98. What is the purpose of the last paragraph?
    A. to explain causes of lack of productivity
    B. to explain why the study was important
    C. to give suggestions to increase work efficiency
    D. to explain the findings of the study

99. According to the passage, why was editing less tiring to workers in Group 2?
    A. Large screens helped them concentrate longer.
    B. They were sitting in a more comfortable position.
    C. Large screens made documents appear more interesting.
    D. They were more familiar with the editing tasks.

The following question refers to two or more sections.

100. How do Sections B and C differ from Section A?
    A. They mention how readers' choices impact the environment.
    B. They provide information about how computers are made.
    C. They discuss what affects workers' comfort.
    D. They assume readers are computer specialists.

End of the Reading and Grammar test.

Writing Test Instructions

This writing test has two parts.

- You have 45 minutes to complete both parts.
- Your responses to both parts should be written in this book.
- You will not be graded on the appearance of your paper, but your handwriting must be readable. You may change or correct your writing, but you should not recopy your entire response.

1. When the examiner tells you to, begin Task 1.
2. When you are done with Task 1, continue on to Task 2.

Do not begin until the examiner tells you to.

Task 1

● **Write sentences to answer the questions.**

1. Do you like to take photographs? What do you take photographs of?

_____

_____

_____

2. Describe a place where you like to take photographs.

_____

_____

_____

3. Tell us about a photograph you took recently.

_____

_____

_____

Writing

● **Write paragraphs to answer the question.**

● **Write about 1 to 2 pages. Your test will be marked down if it is extremely short.**

Some public places have a lot of garbage. One solution is to provide more trash cans for people to use. Another option is to increase penalties for people who throw garbage on the street. What do you think should be done? Use specific examples to support your opinion.

_____

_____

_____

_____

_____

_____

_____

_____

_____

_____

_____

_____

This page is blank.

PRACTICE TEST 3

Listening Section Instructions

In this section of the test, you will show your ability to understand spoken English. There are three parts in this section of the test, with special directions for each part.

Mark your answers in the book. If you do not know the answer, you may guess. Try to answer as many questions as possible.

Part 1

In this part of the test, you will hear short conversations between two people. After each conversation, you will hear a question about it. Choose the best answer to the question from the choices printed in the book. You should mark A, B, C, or D.

There are 19 questions in Part 1. The conversations and questions on the audio will not be repeated. Please listen carefully. Once the audio starts, it will not stop. There is a 12-second pause after each question to give you time to answer.

Do not turn the page until you are told to do so.

Now turn the page.

1. What are the students supposed to do?
   A. write down the most important ideas
   B. write a research paper
   C. talk about what they learned
   D. talk about a different article

2. What does the man think about what the woman said?
   A. He wants to do the same thing.
   B. He is happy that she told him.
   C. He is surprised by it.
   D. He didn't hear her.

3. What does the professor recommend the student do?
   A. research the history of literature
   B. change her major
   C. explain how she became interested in Asia
   D. include other writers in her project

4. Why should the man go early?
   A. because it's a long drive
   B. because he wants a good seat
   C. because the game time changed
   D. because parking is limited

5. What does the woman think about Frank's predictions?
   A. They will be useful for the company.
   B. They are better than hers.
   C. They will please the finance committee.
   D. They are unreasonable.

6. What are the speakers mainly discussing?
   A. where to buy the nicest furniture
   B. the best ways to organize paperwork
   C. how many books the man has
   D. the man's need for a bookcase

7. What will the speakers probably do next?
   A. study alone
   B. arrange a time to meet
   C. meet with their professor
   D. reserve a room at the library

8. How does the woman feel about the trip to San Diego?
   A. It will be more expensive than expected.
   B. A technology specialist must go.
   C. Too many people are going.
   D. They are bringing too many laptops.

9. What is the woman planning to do?
   A. open a new business
   B. ask for identification
   C. make an appointment
   D. get a driver's license

10. Which league did the man ask to join?
    A. the one on Monday
    B. the one on Wednesday
    C. the one on Thursday
    D. the one on Friday

11. What are the speakers commenting on?
    A. parents taking their children to college
    B. participating in an event with many people
    C. giving directions to strangers
    D. former students visiting their college

12. What does the man think about going to the basketball game?
    A. He prefers watching television.
    B. He wants to go but has to work.
    C. He is not interested.
    D. He needs time to think about it.

13. What will the woman do on Tuesday?
    A. email a meeting schedule to the man
    B. arrange a meeting with her coworkers
    C. write a report about a project
    D. take some documents to a meeting

14. What does the woman say about the library?
    A. There aren't enough chairs there.
    B. The chairs there are uncomfortable.
    C. It is too loud.
    D. It is difficult to find.

15. Why did the woman mention a list?
    A. She wants to sign up.
    B. She needs to change her information.
    C. She was not on it.
    D. She wants to be removed from it.

16. What does the woman say about her experiment?
    A. She has written a report of her findings.
    B. The experiment has just been completed.
    C. The results are as she expected.
    D. She is not sure what to do next.

17. What do the speakers agree about?
    A. John has many positive qualities.
    B. John will probably leave the company soon.
    C. They should discuss their concerns with John.
    D. They think John is too young.

18. How do the speakers feel about the new photocopier?
    A. It is too expensive.
    B. It is too big for their office.
    C. It is worse than the old one.
    D. It is more complicated than the old one.

19. Why is the office dark?
    A. It is nighttime.
    B. Someone turned off the lights.
    C. The office lost power.
    D. There is a storm outside.

End of Part 1.

This page is blank.

Part 2

In this part of the test, you will hear longer conversations between two people. After each conversation, you will answer some questions about it. Choose the best answer to the question from the choices printed in the book. You should mark A, B, C, or D.

There are 14 questions in Part 2. The conversations and questions on the audio will not be repeated. If you want to, you may take notes in your book as you listen. Please listen carefully. Once the audio starts, it will not stop. There is a 12-second pause after each question to give you time to answer.

Do not turn the page until you are told to do so.

Now turn the page.

20. What is the woman trying to do?
    A. choose a topic for a research project
    B. decide what to study
    C. make an appointment with her advisor
    D. complete an assignment

21. What does the man say the woman should consider?
    A. when classes are offered
    B. how much time she has to study
    C. what type of job she wants
    D. what her parents think

22. How does the woman feel about her decision?
    A. confused
    B. pressured
    C. hopeful
    D. calm

23. What does the man mean when he says:
    A. He thought she had already made a decision.
    B. He thought she had graduated last semester.
    C. He thought she had finished the required courses.
    D. He thought she already had a job offer.

24. What are the speakers mainly discussing?
    A. where the doctor's office is located
    B. when the man should visit the doctor
    C. the man's health problems
    D. the doctor's schedule

25. What will the man probably do later?
    A. take some medicine
    B. talk with the doctor
    C. check his calendar
    D. go back to the doctor's office

26. What does the woman say might be a problem?
    A. the man getting the flu again
    B. the man's health insurance
    C. paying for the doctor's visit
    D. changing an appointment at the last minute

27. What does the woman want the man to help with?
    A. moving boxes to a new store
    B. placing a large order
    C. finding missing merchandise
    D. delivering packages to customers

28. What is implied about some boxes?
    A. They were sent to the wrong store.
    B. They have been damaged.
    C. They are not big enough.
    D. They are very heavy.

29. Why will the speakers wait to complete a task?
    A. The store is not open yet.
    B. The weather might cause a problem.
    C. The man can't help until later.
    D. The woman can't find a place to park.

30. What does the woman mean when she says: 🔊
    A. The materials are difficult to obtain.
    B. The project details are confusing.
    C. A building is not well constructed.
    D. A schedule is subject to change.

31. What are the speakers mainly discussing?
    A. their friends in London
    B. their upcoming trip to London
    C. where the woman will live in London
    D. where the woman will attend school in London

32. How does the man feel about the woman's preparations?
    A. She has been quite thorough.
    B. She has completed everything quickly.
    C. She is depending too much on friends.
    D. She is waiting too long to make them.

33. What does the woman mean when she says: 🔊
    A. She is nervous about going to London.
    B. She has no friends or relatives in London.
    C. She hopes the man will travel with her.
    D. She thinks London will be lonely.

End of Part 2.

This page is blank.

Part 3

In this part of the test, you will hear some short talks. After each talk, you will answer some questions about it. Choose the best answer to the question from the choices printed in the book. You should mark A, B, C, or D.

There are 17 questions in Part 3. The talks and questions on the audio will not be repeated. If you want to, you may take notes in your book as you listen. Please listen carefully. Once the audio starts, it will not stop. There is a 12-second pause after each question to give you time to answer.

Do not turn the page until you are told to do so.

Now turn the page.

34. What is the research study about?
    A. how perceiving color changes with age
    B. how infants learn to process language
    C. how color is described in different languages
    D. how adults teach infants to name colors

35. What did the people in the research study do?
    A. flash different colored lights on a screen
    B. describe the different colors they saw
    C. use only the left field of vision
    D. look for a flashing circle of light

36. Why does the professor mention Russian speakers?
    A. to discuss changes in Russian descriptions of color
    B. to mention a study with different research findings
    C. to show that research results differed across language groups
    D. to suggest language and perception are connected

37. What does the professor mean when she says:
    A. It's shown the importance of light to color.
    B. It's reminded researchers of the value of color.
    C. It's increased people's understanding of the subject.
    D. It's improved how researchers study light.

38. What is the talk mainly about?
    A. a kind of children's book
    B. the history of storytelling
    C. a new type of picture book
    D. a story about two doors

39. Why does the speaker read to the class?
    A. to introduce a new topic
    B. to demonstrate a good writing technique
    C. to explain the next assignment
    D. to tell them a story

40. What is special about the stories described in the talk?
    A. The plots change based on reader decisions.
    B. They were created by a group of writers.
    C. They are written for adults.
    D. They have no main characters.

41. What does the professor mean when she says:
    A. The cost of children's books has increased.
    B. The stories are like a roller coaster ride.
    C. The stories became less popular.
    D. Some stories are happy and some are sad.

42. What is the speaker's main purpose?

    A. to introduce a new member of the company
    B. to announce a deal between two companies
    C. to discuss the creation of a new department
    D. to explain why the company is moving

43. Which of the following will most likely be a duty of the Transition Task Force?

    A. to decide what roles employees will have
    B. to hire a new Vice President of Finance
    C. to find new clients for the upcoming year
    D. to manage important existing DNJ accounts

44. What major change for DNJ Marketing does the speaker mention?

    A. Publication offices will be moved to another city.
    B. Some employees will be required to relocate.
    C. DNJ Marketing will lay off some employees.
    D. Human Resources will reorganize the departments.

45. Why was Margaret Lomax promoted?

    A. She was a part of the Transition Task Force.
    B. She helped to coordinate the merger.
    C. She made DNJ Marketing successful.
    D. She was an important employee at Bradshire.

46. Why does the speaker say:

    A. to explain what changes will take place in the company
    B. to change the topic of the presentation to company goals
    C. to describe what the company expects the end results to be
    D. to connect the company's goals to plans for achieving them

47. What is the speaker mainly discussing?

    A. the benefits of reusable bottles
    B. why people should volunteer
    C. the results of a community project
    D. a problem in the community

48. What is the speaker's goal?

    A. to explain a project
    B. to tell people to stop using plastic
    C. to raise money for a good cause
    D. to thank volunteers

49. What does the speaker imply about stainless steel drinking bottles?

    A. They are dangerous for people's health.
    B. They are better than plastic bottles.
    C. They are expensive.
    D. They are easy to recycle.

50. What does the man mean when he says:

    A. They will go watch recycling at a plant.
    B. They will only recycle plastic items.
    C. They will put up posters about recycling.
    D. They will make sure bottles are recycled.

End of the Listening test.

This page is blank.

Reading and Grammar Section Instructions

This section of the test focuses on your ability to use English grammar and to understand written English. There are 50 questions in this part of the test. They are numbered 51 to 100.

You will have 65 minutes to complete the entire section. Try to answer all questions. You may answer the questions in any order you wish.

Each question has only one correct answer. Choose the best answer to the question from the choices printed in the book. You should mark A, B, C, or D. If you are not sure about an answer, you may guess.

You may begin now.

GRAMMAR

51. "This is your book, _____?"
   "Yes. I always write my name on the back. See?"
   A. isn't it
   B. this is not
   C. isn't this
   D. is not

52. _____ asked what he was going to do with his bonus money, Bill said he hadn't decided yet.
   A. Despite
   B. When
   C. Although
   D. Because

53. The post office is closed on Sunday, _____ the bank is too.
   A. as
   B. and
   C. also
   D. yet

54. I gave my umbrella to Joe because he didn't have _____.
   A. so
   B. one
   C. some
   D. no

55. _____ criticism of the library is that it is not big enough.
   A. Most commonly
   B. More and more common
   C. The most common
   D. A more commonly

56. _____ with Dr. Morrison's lectures can be very difficult.
   A. Keep up
   B. To keep away
   C. Keeping up
   D. Kept away

57. The school's football team was _____ the state last year.
   A. so much better with
   B. as better for
   C. among the best in
   D. the best one among

58. _____ called for me this afternoon?
   A. Who said you did
   B. Who did you say
   C. Who is saying
   D. Who said

59. If George can run a marathon, I'm sure _____.
   A. I could too
   B. to run too
   C. I could run either
   D. so I could

60. _____ we don't have any additional assignments, we could start preparing for our presentation.
   A. As if
   B. Provided that
   C. Whereas
   D. Even

61. Richard did not mean _____ to sound critical or negative.
    A. his comment being
    B. for his comment
    C. his comment going
    D. that his comment

62. Sarah liked all aspects of the restaurant, but she was _____ the service.
    A. apparently pleasing in
    B. apparently pleased to
    C. especially pleasing for
    D. especially pleased by

63. The budget for building the new city hall was _____ of the previous one.
    A. twice
    B. that twice
    C. the twice
    D. twice that

64. _____ expand, it would probably be able to increase profits.
    A. Were the company to
    B. Has the company
    C. The company could
    D. The company had to

65. It is recommended that every student _____ the first day of class to remain enrolled.
    A. having attended
    B. attend
    C. that attends
    D. attending

66. I'm surprised the dinner turned out so well; I know _____ cooking.
    A. about nothing
    B. nearly nothing
    C. nothing about that
    D. next to nothing about

67. The question as _____ the department will hire more employees is complex.
    A. to whether
    B. of whom
    C. of how
    D. to what

68. _____ two science competitions did Carolyn take time for a vacation.
    A. Only participating
    B. Only after participating in
    C. To have only participated in
    D. Having participated

69. We made Sarah captain because the other team members _____ to her.
    A. look up
    B. will look forward
    C. are looking over
    D. had looked around

70. The manager needs to know _____ precise the new system is.
    A. just how
    B. how just
    C. how is that
    D. that how

Reading and Grammar

READING

This passage is about how people express emotions.

Many of us see the face as a window to a person's emotions. Smiles are generally thought to indicate happiness, and frowns sadness. But expressions aren't the whole story; in fact, they may not even be the key. Contrary to most expectations, new research shows that body language is actually more effective at communicating a person's internal state than facial expressions are.

To test this theory, scientists set up a study to gauge people's ability to read emotion from expressions. The results were intriguing. Participants were shown photos of tennis players who had just won or lost a match and were asked to identify the outcome. It turned out that participants couldn't distinguish winning versus losing unless they could also see the players' bodies. In fact, one group who looked only at the bodies of the players was able to correctly identify the emotion being expressed, yet those seeing only the faces could not.

The researchers then edited the photos, switching the faces so a winner's face was now on a loser's body, and vice versa. Participants still consistently used body language to identify the player's state of mind, whether their facial expression reflected it or not. Yet when these participants were asked, most believed they could successfully use facial expressions to properly identify emotion. The researchers also tested a range of pictures and emotions—pain, sadness, joy—and the results were the same. Of course, expressions do tell us something about how someone is feeling, but paradoxically, when emotions are at their most extreme is when they are hardest to tell apart—just as a cry of pain and a shout of joy often sound similar.

This research could prove useful to people with certain neurological conditions that can make it difficult for them to recognize emotion in others. Typically, training to identify emotions centers on the face, but it may be better to widen that focus so the body and broader environment are part of the picture as well.

71. What is the main conclusion of the research discussed in this passage?
    A. Facial expressions demonstrate internal emotions.
    B. Body language is important in identifying people's emotions.
    C. Some emotions are easier to identify than other ones.
    D. People can learn to recognize emotions by studying photographs.

72. In the last sentence of paragraph 2, what does the word **those** refer to?
    A. faces
    B. participants
    C. emotions
    D. tennis players

73. What does the passage say about the participants' judgments of their own performance?
    A. They underestimated their ability.
    B. They did not correspond with the actual results.
    C. They did not want to evaluate themselves.
    D. They were more accurate than researchers expected.

74. Why does the author mention shouts of joy?
    A. to give an example of a loud sound
    B. to emphasize an argument
    C. to describe what participants studied
    D. to provide a supporting example

75. What is the author's opinion about the research findings discussed in the passage?
    A. They may help some people.
    B. They may confuse some people.
    C. They may not be complete.
    D. They may be too extreme.

This passage is about certain types of fish.

Humans possess only a subset of the sensory abilities that exist in the world of living creatures. There are mammals, for example, that communicate with each other by means of chemicals called pheromones. Some bees see infrared and ultraviolet light. And certain types of fish generate and detect electric fields.

Fish that can both detect and generate electric fields are considered true electric fish; they are *electroreceptive* and *electrogenic*. Those that can perceive electric signals but not produce them, such as sharks and most rays, are not considered true electric fish. Electric fish that can generate an electric discharge powerful enough to stun prey, up to 500 volts, are called strongly electric fish. Examples include the electric eel and electric catfishes. In contrast, weakly electric fish, such as Peters' elephant-nose fish and the black ghost knifefish, generate a discharge that is less than one volt, for the purposes of navigation, object detection, and communication.

The fish's electric output, known as the electric organ discharge—or EOD—is created by a specialized organ that consists of several rows of electrocytes, which are modified muscle or nerve cells usually located in the tail. The signal-emitting organ produces a continuous stream of electrical signals, setting up an electric field around the fish, similar to that surrounding a magnet. To detect these electric signals, electric fish have a large number of electroreceptor cells arranged just under the skin.

Whenever an organism or obstacle comes within range, the electroreceptor cells sense a distortion in the electric field. The fish can determine the characteristics of the object without seeing it, an ability that is especially useful since many are nocturnal and live in murky rivers. They also can modify the shape and intensity of the EOD that they produce in order to signal submission to a larger animal, intimidate rivals, or attract a mate.

76. What is the passage mainly about?
    A. how sensory abilities of humans and fish differ
    B. how some fish produce and use electricity
    C. how electric fish are dangerous to humans and other animals
    D. how electric fish developed their special skills

77. What is the purpose of the first paragraph?
    A. to show that creatures can use senses in different ways
    B. to argue that humans have the most developed senses
    C. to provide examples of senses used for communication
    D. to point out the sensory abilities that are most effective

78. Why are sharks not considered true electric fish?
    A. They use their electric field only for navigation.
    B. They do not use their electric field to catch prey.
    C. They can sense but not create an electric field.
    D. They can emit only a weak electric field.

79. Why are the tails of electric fish important?
    A. They contain cells that protect them from electrical fields.
    B. They are made up of cells that receive electrical signals.
    C. They contain the organ that sends out electrical signals.
    D. They contain a magnetic field.

80. Why does the author mention a magnet?
    A. to explain the nature of the electric field around a fish
    B. to identify an object that blocks the fish's electrical signals
    C. to describe the shape of the electric fish's tail
    D. to show how electric fish avoid electrical signals

A

Pretty Parks Event

Want to help make Centerville even prettier? Join our Pretty Parks Event! We'll be planting cherry and maple trees this fall in South Park.

- All equipment supplied.
- Wear old clothes and dress in multiple layers.
- Lunch and drinks provided.
- Ages 12 and up.
- One free sapling given to each participant—plant a tree in your own yard!

**Saturday, October 28
10 a.m.–3 p.m.**

Participation is free, but registration is required. Call 555-922-1000 to sign up.

B

Paul's Wanderings

www.paultravelsaroundblog.com

April 4

Still in Japan this week, and today was spectacular! My friends invited me to a party in a famous park in Tokyo that's full of cherry trees in bloom right now. This kind of party is called "hanami." One of my friends explained to me that this word basically translates to "looking at flowers." But it's a lot more than just looking at cherry blossoms.

There were dozens of trees in the park full of pink blossoms—and there must have been hundreds of people eating and drinking on blue plastic sheets placed on the ground under the trees. Other people were taking pictures of the flowers. The crowd included families with kids, groups of friends, and coworkers in their company uniforms. In spite of it being completely packed, everyone seemed to be having a great time—it was much livelier than any other picnic I've ever been to. Since the trees only bloom once a year and only last a week or two, it was a good excuse to take a break and enjoy the arrival of spring.

C

An Enduring Gift

For over one hundred years, springtime in Washington, DC, has brought the beauty of thousands of blooming cherry trees bordering the waters of the Tidal Basin and on the grounds of the Washington Monument. A gift from Japan in 1912, the trees were intended to convey the goodwill of the people of Japan to the citizens of the United States. Cherry trees are very important in Japanese culture, where the short-lived beauty of their blossoms represents the cycle of life.

The original gift of two thousand trees, sent in 1909, unfortunately had to be destroyed when it was discovered that they were diseased and carried dangerous insects. To ease an embarrassing diplomatic situation, letters of apology from both sides were exchanged, and a second attempt at the gift was made. Another shipment, this time of three thousand trees, was sent in 1912. These trees had been cultivated in specially created beds to avoid a repeat of the problem with pests and disease.

In 1935, the first official Cherry Blossom Festival was held in Washington, DC. This annual event continues to this day. The dramatic backdrop of the Capitol, the White House, and the monuments that fill the United States' capital city set off the picturesque beauty of the trees, and the Festival draws over a million visitors every year. Its activities include a fireworks display, a parade, and the crowning of a Cherry Blossom Queen.

The U.S. National Park Service has a dedicated team of arborists—tree experts—to care for the cherry trees. Additionally, there are occasional tree-planting events around the city to ensure that, unlike the blossoms themselves, the beauty of Washington, DC's collection of cherry trees lives on.

Refer to page 82 when answering the questions below.

The following questions refer to section A.

81. What should participants do?
    A. bring lunch
    B. wear gloves
    C. bring gardening equipment
    D. wear extra clothes

82. Who is the intended audience for the poster?
    A. people who want to relax in the park
    B. elementary school children
    C. professional gardening companies
    D. people interested in planting trees

The following questions refer to section B.

83. What is the passage mainly about?
    A. a Japanese custom
    B. a type of tree
    C. a company event
    D. an outdoor concert

84. Why did people bring plastic sheets to the park?
    A. to collect cherry blossoms with them
    B. to use when planting cherry trees
    C. to help control the crowd at the party
    D. to set up a picnic on them

85. What would the writer probably suggest about traveling to Tokyo?
    A. It's a good place to see live music.
    B. It's good to visit in the spring.
    C. Families should travel there together.
    D. Visitors should learn some Japanese before going.

The following questions refer to section C.

86. What is the passage mainly about?
    A. the history of Washington, DC
    B. a type of cherry tree
    C. the relationship between Japan and the United States
    D. a famous annual event

87. In the second sentence of paragraph 1, which word could best replace **convey**?
    A. allow
    B. connect
    C. communicate
    D. move

88. Why was a gift of trees given twice?
    A. The first trees turned out to be sick.
    B. The first gift was accidentally returned.
    C. The Americans asked for more trees.
    D. The Japanese had two types of trees to send.

The following questions refer to two or more sections.

89. How does the event in section A differ from those in sections B and C?
    A. It involves more people.
    B. It happens during a different season.
    C. It costs more to participate.
    D. It will take longer to complete.

90. What might the author of section B suggest to visitors at the Cherry Blossom Festival?
    A. have a picnic under the trees
    B. avoid the crowds
    C. set off some fireworks
    D. take a tour of the White House

A | Child Development Class at Lakeview Community Center

Join us at the Lakeview Community Center for a six-week class about early childhood development. The class will provide an overview of the stages of child development and will focus especially on facilitating your child's progress from birth to two years old.

- Sessions led by specialists in the field.
- Educational information provided to take home.
- Join discussion groups with other parents.
- Question-and-answer time after each session.

Meets September 15 – October 31.

Visit us online to learn more and register.

www.lakeviewcommunitycenter.org

B | Class Handout – October 3

Between birth and two years old, children understand the world around them through their senses and physical actions. The influential developmental psychologist Jean Piaget called this the *sensorimotor* stage.

During this time, children begin to understand *object permanence*, which is realizing that objects still exist even if you cannot hear or see them. For example, if you hide a doll behind your back, an infant thinks the doll is completely gone. When the doll reappears, the baby is astonished. As the child develops during the sensorimotor stage, however, she realizes that the doll continues to exist even when she cannot see it.

Another important development at this stage is *intentional action*. For example, a baby might shake a toy that makes a noise he enjoys. He will then intentionally shake the toy again to hear the noise he likes.

Here are some ideas to promote development during this time:

- Play interactive games with your child.
- Let your child play with safe toys that have interesting noises or motions.
- Expose your child to new sights, smells, and textures.

C | Jean Piaget's Contributions to Child Psychology

Jean Piaget, a Swiss educator born in 1896, became interested in child psychology while developing intelligence tests for children in Paris. He noticed that children often answered the same questions incorrectly, which interested him. With a background in natural history and philosophy, Piaget had a scientist's mind, and he wanted to explore what was causing the children to do this.

To better understand their thinking processes, he interviewed hundreds of children and studied their responses. He eventually proposed that children have a very different system of logic and way of considering information than adults do. Previously, people had thought that children processed information in the same way as adults—they just didn't have as much information to process yet. Because of this, teachers often focused on filling children with new information.

Piaget's discoveries emphasized the importance of helping children to develop the structures they use for understanding information. He highlighted the necessity of allowing children to make mistakes and learn from their errors, explaining that this process enables children to develop patterns of learning and discovery.

Piaget went on to define four stages of development in children. Detailing the progression from birth to adulthood, Piaget showed how the mind of a child developed from simply observing to abstract reasoning. He pointed out significant moments in development, such as when a child begins to use symbolism while playing. For example, a child might use a stick and a plastic container to pretend that he is stirring some soup in a pot. This use of symbolism marks an important developmental step.

Piaget's analysis created a new perspective for understanding how children's reasoning develops and laid a foundation of insight that many later researchers built on. His work continues to influence the field of education even today.

Refer to page 84 when answering the questions below.

The following question refers to section A.

91. Who would most likely be interested in this advertisement?
    A. school-age children
    B. high school teachers
    C. parents of babies
    D. community center employees

The following questions refer to section B.

92. What is the purpose of the handout?
    A. to criticize theories of a famous child psychologist
    B. to describe how to keep young children safe when playing
    C. to suggest ways to correct young children's behavior
    D. to discuss early steps in a child's development

93. Why does the passage mention hiding a doll?
    A. to give a negative example of playing
    B. to explain an important concept
    C. to demonstrate what intentional action means
    D. to describe an activity that entertains children

94. According to the passage, what happens when children use intentional action?
    A. They are surprised by adults' interactive games.
    B. They realize that objects they can't see continue to exist.
    C. They hide toys from other children while playing.
    D. They do something to achieve a result.

The following questions refer to section C.

95. What is the main idea of the passage?
    A. Piaget's changes to intelligence tests are still used today.
    B. Piaget's work focused on how children think.
    C. Piaget discovered how adults process information.
    D. Piaget studied child psychology as well as philosophy.

96. According to the passage, how did Piaget primarily study the thought processes of children?
    A. He gave written tests to children.
    B. He asked many children questions.
    C. He observed children playing with their toys.
    D. He read books about child development.

97. Why did Piaget say that children should be allowed to make mistakes?
    A. because it is easier for teachers not to correct them
    B. because they don't usually make many mistakes
    C. because they will become upset if corrected
    D. because it helps them build learning methods

98. Why are a stick and a container mentioned in the passage?
    A. to explain how Piaget studied children
    B. to describe an early stage of development
    C. to give an example of ways to entertain children
    D. to demonstrate the concept of symbolism

99. In the first sentence of paragraph 5, which word could best replace **reasoning**?
    A. playing
    B. thinking
    C. arguing
    D. studying

The following question refers to two or more sections.

100. How can learning about Piaget's stages help parents of young children?
    A. They will better understand changes in their children.
    B. They will share more information with other parents.
    C. They will be able to teach their child to speak.
    D. They will learn to improve their child's health.

End of the Reading and Grammar test.

Writing Test Instructions

This writing test has two parts.

- You have 45 minutes to complete both parts.
- Your responses to both parts should be written in this book.
- You will not be graded on the appearance of your paper, but your handwriting must be readable. You may change or correct your writing, but you should not recopy your entire response.

1. When the examiner tells you to, begin Task 1.
2. When you are done with Task 1, continue on to Task 2.

Do not begin until the examiner tells you to.

Task 1

- **Write sentences to answer the questions.**

1. What do/did you like studying at school? How long did you study it for?

_____

_____

_____

2. What do/did you like about that subject and why?

_____

_____

_____

3. Tell us about what you have learned studying that subject.

_____

_____

_____

Writing

Task 2

- **Write paragraphs to answer the question.**
- **Write about 1 to 2 pages. Your test will be marked down if it is extremely short.**

Some schools require their students to wear uniforms while others do not. What are the advantages and disadvantages of students wearing uniforms to school? Use specific examples to support your ideas.

_____

_____

_____

_____

_____

_____

_____

_____

_____

_____

_____

_____

_____

This page is blank.

PRACTICE TEST 4

Listening

Listening Section Instructions

In this section of the test, you will show your ability to understand spoken English. There are three parts in this section of the test, with special directions for each part.

Mark your answers in the book. If you do not know the answer, you may guess. Try to answer as many questions as possible.

Part 1

In this part of the test, you will hear short conversations between two people. After each conversation, you will hear a question about it. Choose the best answer to the question from the choices printed in the book. You should mark A, B, C, or D.

There are 19 questions in Part 1. The conversations and questions on the audio will not be repeated. Please listen carefully. Once the audio starts, it will not stop. There is a 12-second pause after each question to give you time to answer.

Do not turn the page until you are told to do so.

Now turn the page.

1. What will the woman probably do?

   A. order the book

   B. go to another store

   C. send a book to the man

   D. drop the class

2. What problem does the woman have?

   A. She isn't sure what the sweater costs.

   B. The website isn't working.

   C. She ordered the wrong item.

   D. The catalog she has isn't current.

3. How does the man feel?

   A. tired

   B. excited

   C. anxious

   D. disappointed

4. Why did the man talk to the professor?

   A. He did not understand the lecture.

   B. He wants to get some class material.

   C. He does not know her office hours.

   D. He wants help preparing for an exam.

5. What will the man probably do?

   A. schedule a conference call

   B. meet with the woman in the morning

   C. leave work earlier than usual

   D. make a doctor's appointment

6. What does the man suggest the woman do?

   A. change the bank that she uses

   B. refuse to pay the late fee

   C. arrange for her bills to be paid automatically

   D. mail in her payment immediately

7. Why is the woman meeting the dean?

   A. to ask for funding for the sports club

   B. to choose a new student government representative

   C. to arrange a tour for new students

   D. to present more information about a program

8. What will the woman probably do?

   A. request an OfficePro catalog

   B. ask why prices have been raised

   C. contact Taylor Office Supply

   D. send payment for an order

9. What can be inferred about the woman?

   A. She doesn't think the movie is funny.

   B. She'll try to buy a ticket later.

   C. She doesn't want to see the movie.

   D. She'll watch the movie today.

10. How has the man helped the woman?

    A. by recommending her for a job

    B. by suggesting she contact a professional group

    C. by suggesting a different newspaper

    D. by encouraging her to change her career

11. What does the man want to know?
    A. what the course focuses on
    B. what the course will cost
    C. when the course begins
    D. what the woman learned

12. What does the woman suggest the man do?
    A. clean his glasses
    B. buy an extra pair of glasses
    C. return the glasses
    D. wear different glasses for reading

13. What was John's concern?
    A. He might not like his new job.
    B. He might have to get a second job.
    C. He might not get the job he wanted.
    D. He might not get a well-paid job.

14. Why did the woman talk to the man?
    A. to motivate him to attend class
    B. to warn him about the exams
    C. to encourage him to talk in class
    D. to give him a new discussion topic

15. What does the woman want to know?
    A. who forced the mayor to quit
    B. what the man's qualifications are
    C. who will replace the mayor
    D. what the man thinks about the situation

16. What will the woman probably do?
    A. attend college with her boss
    B. pay for the class by herself
    C. move to another department
    D. create a department website

17. Why is the man upset?
    A. He has to look for another buyer.
    B. He has to negotiate with the couple.
    C. He accepted a low price for the house.
    D. He decided not to sell the house.

18. What are the woman's expectations for the race?
    A. She probably won't finish it.
    B. She doesn't think she'll win it.
    C. She'll perform better than her last one.
    D. She thinks it takes too long to do.

19. What does the woman say about the figures?
    A. She thinks they are incomplete.
    B. She doubts their accuracy.
    C. She thinks they are correct.
    D. She wants the man to check them.

End of Part 1.

This page is blank.

Part 2

In this part of the test, you will hear longer conversations between two people. After each conversation, you will answer some questions about it. Choose the best answer to the question from the choices printed in the book. You should mark A, B, C, or D.

There are 14 questions in Part 2. The conversations and questions on the audio will not be repeated. If you want to, you may take notes in your book as you listen. Please listen carefully. Once the audio starts, it will not stop. There is a 12-second pause after each question to give you time to answer.

Do not turn the page until you are told to do so.

Now turn the page.

20. Why is the man visiting the woman?
    A. to help her clean up the apartment
    B. to help her pack her boxes
    C. to find out what the rent costs
    D. to look at her apartment

21. What does the man describe as a cave?
    A. the stack of boxes
    B. the subway he took to get there
    C. the woman's apartment
    D. an apartment he saw earlier

22. What is NOT included in the monthly rent?
    A. gas
    B. electric
    C. water
    D. trash collection

23. According to the woman, what will happen soon?
    A. New carpet will be installed.
    B. She will move in to the apartment.
    C. The apartment will be cleaned.
    D. The apartment will be painted.

24. What is the student discussing with the professor?
    A. how to organize her notes
    B. a homework problem
    C. an upcoming exam
    D. topics for a project

25. What does the professor say about the course content?
    A. It is unusually difficult.
    B. It is not the same every year.
    C. It is unfamiliar to many students.
    D. It is based on the textbook.

26. What does the professor suggest that the student do?
    A. review the syllabus
    B. take a different class
    C. buy a different textbook
    D. take better notes

27. What does the woman recommend that the man do?
    A. buy a warranty
    B. read about laptop computers
    C. ask someone for advice
    D. pay extra for a larger hard drive

28. What happened to the woman's computer?
    A. She had to replace it.
    B. She had to find another one.
    C. The hard drive failed.
    D. It was stolen.

29. How does the man feel about buying a computer?
    A. overwhelmed
    B. surprised
    C. disappointed
    D. excited

30. What does the woman mean when she says:
    A. The computer will not have problems.
    B. The man can fix the computer himself.
    C. The woman will fix the man's computer.
    D. The computer repairs will not cost money.

31. What are the speakers talking about?
    A. replacing a retiring coworker
    B. training a new staff member
    C. interviewing a newspaper reporter
    D. writing their job descriptions

32. Why will the woman talk to Human Resources?
    A. to learn how to advertise the position
    B. to find out when she can start holding interviews
    C. to learn what her new responsibilities are
    D. to ask how long the training should last

33. What does the man say he wants to do?
    A. ask Mary to train Stuart
    B. interview Mary before meeting Stuart
    C. talk to Stuart about what his job duties are
    D. have Stuart start the new job soon

End of Part 2.

This page is blank.

Part 3

In this part of the test, you will hear some short talks. After each talk, you will answer some questions about it. Choose the best answer to the question from the choices printed in the book. You should mark A, B, C, or D.

There are 17 questions in Part 3. The talks and questions on the audio will not be repeated. If you want to, you may take notes in your book as you listen. Please listen carefully. Once the audio starts, it will not stop. There is a 12-second pause after each question to give you time to answer.

Do not turn the page until you are told to do so.

Now turn the page.

34. What was the research study about?
   A. how often teenagers use a computer
   B. where teenagers buy their CDs
   C. what kind of music teenagers like
   D. how teenagers use the internet for music

35. How was the information for the study collected?
   A. live interviews
   B. email questionnaires
   C. telephone surveys
   D. website forms

36. What does the speaker say about teenage girls who spend a lot of time online?
   A. They spend lots of money on music magazines.
   B. They often use the internet to buy their music.
   C. They like buying music at the store.
   D. They attend a lot of live concerts.

37. What kind of people tend to be music influencers?
   A. teens who watch a lot of music videos
   B. teenage boys who spend a lot of money on music
   C. teenage girls who often listen to music
   D. teenage boys who download music from the internet

38. What will the ID cards be used for?
   A. accessing the employee lounge
   B. turning off the alarm system
   C. recording hours worked
   D. logging on to company computers

39. When will the employees swipe their cards?
   A. when entering or exiting the building
   B. when receiving their paychecks
   C. when paying for their lunches
   D. when locking the office doors

40. After the talk was finished, what did the speaker expect the audience to do?
   A. come pick up their cards from her
   B. start practicing how to use the system
   C. try to lock and unlock the door
   D. ask her some questions

41. Why does the woman say:
   A. to show the employees a picture of the new ID cards
   B. to check that the employees have the new work manual
   C. to demonstrate the new card reader for the employees
   D. to make sure the employees understand the new system

42. What is the speaker's main purpose?
    A. to convince people to join a tour
    B. to thank people for taking a tour
    C. to explain how to take part in a tour
    D. to prepare people for a tour

43. What is the main focus of the tour?
    A. a modern architectural style
    B. villas built after 1871
    C. several older buildings
    D. homes with simple interiors

44. Why does the speaker mention Chicago's Great Fire?
    A. to emphasize two different architectural periods
    B. to explain the origins of Italianate architecture
    C. to describe when the population of Chicago grew
    D. to show when the first buildings were erected

45. According to the speaker, what will the people do on the tour?
    A. meet some local architects
    B. see a building under construction
    C. stop at the city's tallest building
    D. visit homes of a certain style

46. What does the speaker mean when she says: 🔊
    A. The roofs are very distinctive.
    B. The roofs come in several different styles.
    C. The roofs are inexpensive to maintain.
    D. The roofs are very colorful.

47. What is the speaker's main purpose?
    A. to prepare students for tomorrow's class
    B. to help students understand climate change
    C. to encourage students to attend a lecture
    D. to explain an article the students have read

48. Why does the speaker think the event will interest the students?
    A. They will write a paper on climate change.
    B. Dr. Willis is a famous philosopher.
    C. They will study ethics later.
    D. Dr. Willis will meet with them individually.

49. What does the speaker say about future generations of human beings?
    A. People today have responsibilities toward them.
    B. They will have the same problems as people today.
    C. Their lives may be more difficult than people's today.
    D. They will find a solution to climate change.

50. What can be inferred about the speaker and Dr. Willis?
    A. They know each other personally.
    B. They hold some similar opinions.
    C. They have degrees in philosophy.
    D. They have written about climate change.

End of the Listening test.

This page is blank.

Reading and Grammar Section Instructions

This section of the test focuses on your ability to use English grammar and to understand written English. There are 50 questions in this part of the test. They are numbered 51 to 100.

You will have 65 minutes to complete the entire section. Try to answer all questions. You may answer the questions in any order you wish.

Each question has only one correct answer. Choose the best answer to the question from the choices printed in the book. You should mark A, B, C, or D. If you are not sure about an answer, you may guess.

You may begin now.

GRAMMAR

51. When you go to the supermarket, can you
    _____ paper towels for me?
    A. pick up some
    B. pick on some
    C. pick at those
    D. pick off those

52. Houses in rural areas generally cost ten percent
    less _____ the state.
    A. than in the rest of
    B. than for the rest
    C. with the rest of
    D. of the rest

53. To remain competitive, _____ did we lower
    prices, but we also extended the store's hours.
    A. if simply
    B. even though
    C. still never
    D. not only

54. Karen _____ from Austin to San Antonio even
    though it was only 75 miles.
    A. flown
    B. flew
    C. fly
    D. flies

55. The deadline _____ term papers is Friday,
    next week.
    A. submitting
    B. to be submitted
    C. for submitting
    D. for to submit

56. When we next meet, I'd like to ask you _____
    you think about the ending of the novel.
    A. how would
    B. why will
    C. which
    D. what

57. I sent the wrong file with my last email; please
    use _____ this message instead.
    A. the one attached to
    B. the attached one
    C. one attached at
    D. one of the attached

58. Every small business needs to have a system
    in place _____ expenses.
    A. keeping track
    B. for keeping track
    C. keep track of
    D. to keep track of

59. To cut costs, many universities are now charging
    students a fee _____ paper copies of their
    grades.
    A. to be mailed them
    B. to mail them
    C. mailing to them
    D. mailing for them

60. After he started cycling, Mike soon became as
    fit as he _____ in his life.
    A. will ever have
    B. had to
    C. had ever been
    D. always has been

61. _____ I take two extra classes this semester, I will not be able to graduate this year.
    A. In case
    B. In the event
    C. Except that
    D. Unless

62. Brazilian soccer fans _____ more than $16 billion annually on soccer-related merchandise.
    A. reportedly spend
    B. are reportedly spent
    C. reportedly spending
    D. reportedly has spent

63. The quality of the singing _____ people of all ages enjoyed the concert.
    A. was that
    B. was such
    C. was such that
    D. so that

64. I did not trust his plans for developing the new product, nor _____ at first.
    A. did our boss trust
    B. did our boss
    C. our boss trusted
    D. our boss had

65. This student's research is important _____ proves our previous findings were not correct.
    A. so that it
    B. that it
    C. such as that
    D. in that it

66. When you buy a car, there are many things to consider _____ just the price.
    A. without
    B. apart
    C. other
    D. besides

67. Even if I had agreed to help you with your essay, I _____ finished it by tomorrow.
    A. cannot have
    B. could not have
    C. could not
    D. cannot

68. Building a new factory was expensive, but it is _____ worthwhile.
    A. proved to be
    B. proved being
    C. proving to have been
    D. proven to being

69. Unfortunately, he has made _____ progress on his project over the past year.
    A. none at all
    B. no or less
    C. little to no
    D. little less

70. Carla is someone _____ to get up early in the morning.
    A. she doesn't like
    B. who doesn't like
    C. isn't she liking
    D. that isn't liking

READING

This passage is about speech research.

Involving several parts of the body, the production of the human voice is a complicated process. Besides the larynx, colloquially called the *voice box*, speech involves the lungs, vocal chords, tongue, lips, and various muscles. Because of this, addressing issues with voice production is a challenging task. Studies of how sound is produced in two distinct styles of singing provides insight into how certain voice issues could be helped.

In classical Western singing, vocalists can vary the pitch of their voices—the notes that they hit—using a technique called *vibrato*. But in traditional Hindustani singing, vocalists consciously and rapidly fluctuate their pitch using *taan*. While vibrato produces a smooth flow between notes, taan's changes in pitch are abrupt. By connecting both types of singers to equipment that measures air flow and the frequency of the opening and closing of the vocal cords, speech researchers collect data that demonstrate how both voluntary and involuntary pitch changes occur. Researchers want to better understand the physiological differences in how vibrato and taan are produced. Once these differences are more thoroughly understood, they expect this knowledge to be useful in several contexts.

For example, researchers are hopeful about gaining more insight into how the physical aspects of voice production are related to vocal longevity—why some vocalists can perform well for decades, while others lose their abilities within just a few years. There is also potential to help speech therapists design effective treatments for speech problems stemming from illness. Those for whom speech is important to their work—such as actors, singers, and teachers—could be helped to vary, strengthen, and repair their voices. Since not everyone produces a given sound the same way, comparative studies of voices are a promising means of providing alternate models of sound production.

71. What is the main purpose of the passage?
    A. to demonstrate differences in Western and Hindustani singing
    B. to show techniques for assessing voice patterns
    C. to explain why people lose their voices
    D. to introduce possible applications for voice research

72. Why does the author mention the larynx?
    A. to mention why people have speech problems
    B. to introduce what is necessary for speech
    C. to describe how it functions
    D. to explain why it's called the voice box

73. According to the passage, why is addressing problems with voice production difficult?
    A. Not much is known about these problems.
    B. People use their voices differently.
    C. Many people are too old to be helped.
    D. It is a complex process using many body parts.

74. In the third sentence of paragraph 2, what does the word **abrupt** mean?
    A. continuous
    B. sudden
    C. concise
    D. brief

75. What are the researchers' feelings about the research?
    A. They are optimistic that it can help people.
    B. They think they have discovered the key to vocal longevity.
    C. They find the results to be contradictory.
    D. They think it is not producing results.

This passage is about drilling for oil.

As early as the 1890s, crude oil was being pumped from wells drilled into the seabed off the coast of California. Since then, public demand for oil and gasoline has caused oil companies to drill farther and farther offshore. To do so, they have faced numerous challenges, first in locating underwater oil reserves and second in drilling down and safely extracting the oil from these sources.

The search for oil fields on land relies on geological studies and exploration seismology, which use either small explosions or a truck-mounted vibrating mechanism to generate waves that reverberate back from the different rock layers below. Offshore, similar techniques are used. Once a promising area has been determined, bursts of compressed air are released into the water from a ship above. This creates sound waves that travel through the Earth's crust and then bounce back to listening devices pulled behind the ship. In both types of locations, computer programs interpret the resulting data and guide the selection of locations for the placement of drills.

Initially, for drilling and production in relatively shallow waters, companies built fixed platforms on the seabed. For oil fields up to 120 meters deep, they had platforms constructed and towed into place, with long pillars inserted into the ocean floor. Beginning in 1967, for depths to about 1,200 meters, floating platforms were towed into position and anchored with cables. In the decades that followed, oil production worldwide has moved into even deeper waters. In fact, deepwater drilling more than tripled since the year 2000. As world energy demands increase and drilling technology advances, there is growing interest in offshore oil exploration in areas that were previously considered too challenging to access, too environmentally delicate, or not potentially profitable enough.

Because of the risks inherent in deepwater drilling, the use of robotics on offshore oil platforms is increasing. However, it remains a difficult enterprise, with many safety and environmental issues posed by the remote and often harsh conditions.

76. In the last sentence of paragraph 1, which of the phrases could replace **extracting**?
    A. getting around
    B. clearing away
    C. getting to
    D. taking out

77. According to the passage, how is the search for oil offshore different from the search on land?
    A. in what is discovered in the various rock layers
    B. in the scientists who carry out the studies
    C. in the quality of oil that is discovered
    D. in the way waves are created

78. According to the passage, what happened in 2000?
    A. Oil companies started to use robots to drill for oil.
    B. Oil production in deep waters started to increase significantly.
    C. There were several safety incidents with offshore drilling.
    D. Geologists began to use new wave technology for locating oil fields.

79. What does paragraph 3 suggest about areas with unique or fragile ecosystems?
    A. They have been seriously damaged by oil drilling.
    B. They are no longer used for oil drilling.
    C. They may be increasingly explored for oil.
    D. They may not have many oil fields.

80. What is the purpose of the final paragraph?
    A. to express doubts about the wisdom of offshore oil production
    B. to indicate continued challenges in offshore oil production
    C. to summarize the accomplishments of offshore oil production
    D. to explore the environmental effect of offshore oil production

A

Eagle Chocolate's Ultimate Decadence Bar

You are invited to try a free sample of the Ultimate Decadence Bar. It's the chocolate lover's new bar of choice.

To create the world's most delicious chocolate bar, we use only the finest chocolate and other ingredients. South American cocoa and Caribbean sugar are blended to create the highest quality dark chocolate bar available.

Go ahead, indulge in the Ultimate Decadence – you deserve it!

Stop by the Eagle Chocolate Store and try one today!

B

Good News for Chocolate Lovers!

Recent research shows that eating moderate amounts of chocolate may be good for you.

Several studies published in the last few months point to the health benefits in cocoa and other chocolates. These include keeping hearts healthy by lowering high blood pressure and maintaining healthy blood flow.

Cocoa contains a substance that seems to help the body regulate nitric oxide levels, which are crucial to controlling blood flow and blood pressure. Cocoa beans also contain large amounts of compounds called flavanols. These plant compounds offer strong antioxidant properties and can prevent fats in the bloodstream from oxidizing. This helps reduce the potential for clogged arteries—a major contributor to heart disease.

Dark chocolate contains more flavanols than milk chocolate or other kinds of processed chocolate, such as chocolate syrups or cocoa powder. This is because flavanols are destroyed or removed in processing. Dark chocolate is a less-refined product, therefore retaining more flavanols than other kinds of chocolates.

C

Can an Industry be Trusted to Research Itself?

Over the past few years, much research has been focused on the purported health benefits of eating chocolate. Many studies have indicated that cocoa, the principal component of all chocolate, has many health benefits, especially regarding cardiovascular health.

One major problem with the research is that most of it comes from the Cocoa Research Institute (CRI), a research institute funded almost entirely by cocoa producers and candy manufacturers. The obvious question is: Why should we trust the data about a product that has been funded by the industry that produces it?

"That's an excellent question, and one we hear all the time," said Dr. Lyle Stemple, director of research at the CRI. "But if the industry hadn't backed the research, then it probably never would have been done. The fact that the industry paid for the research doesn't automatically invalidate it. Almost every study we've put out has been later replicated by other independent research groups. Generally they've obtained similar results."

Dr. Stemple compared the situation to that of the oat industry funding research showing how oats lower cholesterol. Another example is soy farmers who funded early studies that indicated proteins and antioxidants in soy products might help heart disease. Independent research done by labs around the world confirmed these conclusions, and led to further research that has greatly expanded upon the early work.

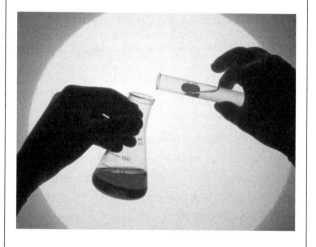

Refer to page 108 when answering the questions below.

The following questions refer to section A.

81. What is the purpose of the advertisement?
    A. to describe where a new product is made
    B. to explain how to buy a new product
    C. to offer customers a discount on a new product
    D. to encourage people to taste a new product

82. What features of the product are described in the advertisement?
    A. the excellent ingredients
    B. the low cost
    C. the health benefits
    D. the beautiful packaging

The following questions refer to section B.

83. In the first sentence of paragraph 3, which word can replace **regulate**?
    A. produce
    B. digest
    C. remove
    D. adjust

84. According to the passage, what is one health benefit of flavanols?
    A. They help the body absorb vitamins and minerals.
    B. They reduce nitric oxide levels in the blood.
    C. They help reduce the risk of heart disease.
    D. They aid in eliminating harmful substances from the body.

85. What is implied about milk chocolate?
    A. The milk helps boost its health benefits.
    B. It is less refined than chocolate syrups or cocoa powder.
    C. It contains less nitric oxide than dark chocolate.
    D. The process that creates it lowers its flavanol content.

The following questions refer to section C.

86. In the first sentence of paragraph 1, why does the author refer to the health benefits of eating chocolate as **purported**?
    A. There is strong evidence to support them.
    B. They are short term.
    C. They are not commonly known.
    D. There is doubt about them.

87. According to the article, what problem is associated with research on cocoa?
    A. Much of the research is not done independently.
    B. The research is very expensive to conduct.
    C. Food product research is not respected by scientists.
    D. Much of the research has not yet been replicated.

88. In the last sentence of paragraph 2, what does **it** refer to?
    A. a question
    B. the industry
    C. a product
    D. an institute

89. Why are soy farmers mentioned in the article?
    A. to illustrate how an industry funded its own research
    B. to explain when research on the health benefits of food began
    C. to contrast soy farmers with chocolate manufacturers
    D. to describe how antioxidants in soy products have increased

The following question refers to two or more sections.

90. What can be inferred about the studies on flavanols in cocoa?
    A. They are based on studies of flavanols in soy and oats.
    B. They were probably done by the CRI.
    C. They did not include Eagle Chocolate products.
    D. They have been challenged by independent research groups.

A

Queenstown Balloon Festival at Bennett Airport

The festival is open to the public
FREE OF CHARGE

Schedule of Events

Friday, September 19
6:00 p.m. .... Launch of 40 hot air balloons, including some special-shape balloons

Saturday, September 20
9:30 a.m. .... Flight of 50 balloons
12:30–4:30 p.m. Balloon Festival Art Show, kite flying, & military aircraft display
6:00 p.m. .... Launch of 75 hot air balloons, including some special shapes
8:30 p.m. .... Fireworks display

Sunday, September 21
11:30 a.m. .... Launch of 90 balloons
4:00 p.m. .... Launch of 25 hot air balloons, including some special shapes

Please keep in mind that:
All balloon flights are subject to cancellation due to wind, lightning, etc.

Dogs are not allowed in the festival.

B

Crossing the Atlantic in a Hot Air Balloon

Hot air balloons have been around since the late 18th century, but no one crossed the Atlantic Ocean in one until 1987.

Two balloonists, Richard Branson of England and Per Lindstrand of Sweden, set off from Maine in the United States on July 2, 1987. Their destination was Scotland, 3,400 miles away. Their balloon was as tall as a 22-story building and could hold 2.3 million cubic feet of air. It was the largest balloon ever flown up to that point. The large capacity allowed them to travel extremely fast; in under 32 hours they crossed the ocean and were over Northern Ireland.

The balloon experienced rough weather over Northern Ireland and accidentally touched ground, but just for a few seconds. The men managed to get the craft back up and were heading towards Scotland again when the weather worsened. They had to abandon the balloon over the North Channel, the body of water separating Northern Ireland and Scotland. Both men jumped out and were rescued by the Royal Navy.

It was later decided that even though they did not make it to their final destination, since they did "land" in Northern Ireland, their voyage was a successful Atlantic balloon crossing.

C

Using Balloons to Collect Data on the Stratosphere

Balloons launched into the stratosphere in effect put a laboratory in the sky, allowing active chemical substances to reveal themselves in situ. These atoms and molecules—*species*, as we shall call them—are mostly of types so active that they cannot be touched without disappearing. One cannot open a bottle at high altitude and bring these unstable gases back to the lab for analysis because they would instantly combine with the bottle wall. One must instead take the lab to the gases—and take care as well that the lab itself not interfere with the species' normal activities.

For example, in a test for ClO^- (chlorine and oxygen atoms joined in unstable pairs that attack oxygen atoms, which are the raw material of ozone), a balloon is launched, and as it falls, ink traces appear on four paper tapes at a monitoring site on the ground. These provide rough profiles of the incoming data, which are also being displayed in digital form on nearby monitors. The data are generated as test devices on the balloon count molecules by means of a technique called *resonance fluorescence*. The two pods of test instruments are sniffing for molecules of ClO^- using two different methods. Because ClO^- is present only at a level of about 100 parts per trillion, accuracy of instruments is critical and redundancy of readings is desirable. The two methods of arriving at one kind of information will, it is hoped, confirm one another and lend confidence in the remotely gathered data.

Refer to page 110 when answering the questions below.

The following question refers to section A.

91. What warning is included in the schedule?
    A. There is a charge to attend the events.
    B. The event location is subject to change.
    C. Weather conditions could affect the events.
    D. Many visitors will bring their dogs.

The following questions refer to section B.

92. Why does the writer compare the balloon to a building?
    A. to explain how it was designed
    B. to show how big it was
    C. to explain why it crashed
    D. to show how far it had to travel

93. How did the men's trip end?
    A. They landed on a navy ship.
    B. They disembarked in Northern Ireland.
    C. They were pulled from the water by rescuers.
    D. Their craft fell apart over Scotland.

94. Based on the passage, how could the men be described?
    A. as sailors
    B. as tourists
    C. as adventurers
    D. as inventors

The following questions refer to section C.

95. What does the author say the balloons in the passage are like?
    A. laboratories
    B. monitors
    C. unstable chemicals
    D. workers

96. Why are the data collected in the stratosphere?
    A. The species involved are unstable.
    B. The species involved are rare.
    C. The species involved cannot be made in a lab.
    D. The species involved combine with gases there.

97. According to the passage, what should be avoided in these kinds of experiments?
    A. redundancy of readings
    B. attacking oxygen atoms
    C. destroying the ozone
    D. disturbing the species' behavior

98. In the third sentence of paragraph 2, which word is closest in meaning to **generated**?
    A. affected
    B. experimented
    C. produced
    D. noticed

99. What is resonance fluorescence used for?
    A. to count molecules
    B. to collect molecules
    C. to combine chemicals
    D. to correct for inaccurate data

The following question refers to two or more sections.

100. What can be inferred from the three passages?
    A. Balloons have increased in popularity over the last 200 years.
    B. People traveling in balloons should not conduct experiments.
    C. Many experiments are conducted at balloon festivals.
    D. Balloons have both recreational and scientific uses.

End of the Reading and Grammar test.

Writing Test Instructions

This writing test has two parts.

- You have 45 minutes to complete both parts.
- Your responses to both parts should be written in this book.
- You will not be graded on the appearance of your paper, but your handwriting must be readable. You may change or correct your writing, but you should not recopy your entire response.

1. When the examiner tells you to, begin Task 1.
2. When you are done with Task 1, continue on to Task 2.

Do not begin until the examiner tells you to.

Task 1

- **Write sentences to answer the questions.**

1. What is your favorite place to travel? How often have you been there?

_____

_____

_____

2. What do you like about it and why?

_____

_____

_____

3. Tell us about the last time you went there.

_____

_____

_____

Writing

Task 2

- ● **Write paragraphs to answer the question.**
- ● **Write about 1 to 2 pages. Your test will be marked down if it is extremely short.**

In some cities, local governments provide support for public art, such as fountains and sculptures. Many people think this makes cities more appealing, but others think the funds would be better spent in other ways. What do you think? Give reasons to support your opinion.

This page is blank.

SPEAKING PRACTICE TEST PROMPTS

Test 1

Part 1

In this part of the test, you will describe a picture and complete some tasks. You will have 60 seconds to respond to each task.

TASK 1.   [60 seconds]

Describe the beach.

TASK 2.   [60 seconds]

Tell me about what you do when you relax outside.

TASK 3.   [60 seconds]

Some people think spending time outside helps us relax and stay healthy. How do you feel after you spend time outside? Explain your answer.

Part 2

In this part of the test, you will complete two different tasks. You will be told when to begin speaking. You will have 90 seconds to respond to each task.

TASK 4.   [90 seconds]

Your friend is thinking about leaving college so he can play music full-time. He wants to take time to travel with his rock band while he is still young. What are the advantages and disadvantages of this idea?

TASK 5.   [90 seconds]

The number of students at a local school has grown. Some teachers have suggested moving the students to a new school building to solve this problem. Many parents think this is a bad idea. I am the school principal. Tell me what you think about this idea and try to convince me to agree with you.

Part 1

In this part of the test, you will describe a picture and complete some tasks. You will have 60 seconds to respond to each task.

TASK 1. [60 seconds]

Describe the sporting event.

TASK 2. [60 seconds]

Tell me about a time when you watched a sporting event.

TASK 3. [60 seconds]

Some people enjoy team sports. Others prefer to simply exercise by themselves. Which do you prefer? Give your opinion and reasons to support it.

Part 2

In this part of the test, you will complete two different tasks. You will be told when to begin speaking. You will have 90 seconds to respond to each task.

TASK 4. [90 seconds]

A friend of yours wants to get a second college degree and would like your advice. Your friend is considering attending a small local school instead of an expensive, well-known university. What are the advantages and disadvantages of this idea?

TASK 5. [90 seconds]

The principal at the local high school is considering adding cooking classes to replace some traditional science classes. She wants to educate all young people about eating healthy foods. I am a member of the school board. Tell me what you think about this idea and try to convince me to agree with you.

Test 3

Part 1

In this part of the test, you will describe a picture and complete some tasks. You will have 60 seconds to respond to each task.

TASK 1. [60 seconds]

Describe the airport.

TASK 2. [60 seconds]

Tell me about the last time you traveled somewhere.

TASK 3. [60 seconds]

Some people like traveling. Other people prefer to stay home. How do you feel about traveling? Give your opinion and reasons to support it.

Speaking Practice Test

Part 2

In this part of the test, you will complete two different tasks. You will be told when to begin speaking. You will have 90 seconds to respond to each task.

TASK 4. [90 seconds]

My town is hosting a music festival this spring. Many university students would like to work at the festival. What are the advantages and disadvantages of hiring students to do this work?

TASK 5. [90 seconds]

To improve teenagers' health, the school board wants to add mandatory exercise classes every day. Some people think this is a bad idea because there would be less time for other subjects. I work for the school board. Tell me what you think about this proposal and convince me to agree with you.

Test 4

Part 1

In this part of the test, you will describe a picture and complete some tasks. You will have 60 seconds to respond to each task.

TASK 1. [60 seconds]

Describe the family meal.

TASK 2. [60 seconds]

Tell me about a meal that you really enjoyed.

TASK 3. [60 seconds]

Some people like to eat at home. Other people like to go to restaurants. What do you prefer to do? Give your opinion and reasons to support it.

Part 2

In this part of the test, you will complete two different tasks. You will be told when to begin speaking. You will have 90 seconds to respond to each task.

TASK 4. [90 seconds]

The local school board is thinking of reducing the hours that children spend in school from 7 hours a day to 4 hours a day in order to save money. What are the advantages and disadvantages of this idea?

TASK 5. [90 seconds]

Parents in your community want to become involved in their children's education. They want to teach in the schools even though they don't have teaching experience. Some teachers do not like this idea. I'm a member of the school board. Tell me what you think about this and try to convince me to agree with you.

The following pages provide a space to record your practice test results and take notes that will help you prepare for future practice tests and the actual test. Use Self-Assessment and Review charts to take notes on vocabulary and grammar from the Listening and Reading sections that you want to study and to generate topic outlines and examples to practice your writing and speaking. Your teacher will have specific suggestions to help you.

Multiple Choice Sections

Practice Test	Date Taken	Test Section	Score (Number Correct)	Estimated CEFR Level	Notes
1		Listening			
		Reading			
Personal goals for Practice Test 2:					
2		Listening			
		Reading			
Personal goals for Practice Test 3:					
3		Listening			
		Reading			
Personal goals for Practice Test 4:					
4		Listening			
		Reading			

Writing and Speaking Sections

Practice Test	Date Taken	Test Section	Teacher Feedback	Notes
1		Writing		
		Speaking		
Personal goals for Practice Test 2:				
2		Writing		
		Speaking		
Personal goals for Practice Test 3:				
3		Writing		
		Speaking		
Personal goals for Practice Test 4:				
4		Writing		
		Speaking		

Practice Test 1: Self-Assessment and Review

Vocabulary to Study			

Grammar Items/Examples to Study			

Writing Practice

Topic:

Key vocabulary:

Outline of main ideas:

Notes/details/supporting examples:

Speaking Practice

Topic:

Key vocabulary:

Outline of main ideas:

Notes/details/supporting examples:

Practice Test 2: Self-Assessment and Review

Vocabulary to Study

Grammar Items/Examples to Study

Writing Practice

Topic:

Key vocabulary:

Outline of main ideas:

Notes/details/supporting examples:

Speaking Practice

Topic:

Key vocabulary:

Outline of main ideas:

Notes/details/supporting examples:

Practice Test 3: Self-Assessment and Review

Vocabulary to Study

Grammar Items/Examples to Study

Writing Practice

Topic:

Key vocabulary:

Outline of main ideas:

Notes/details/supporting examples:

Speaking Practice

Topic:

Key vocabulary:

Outline of main ideas:

Notes/details/supporting examples:

Practice Test 4: Self-Assessment and Review

Vocabulary to Study

Grammar Items/Examples to Study

Writing Practice

Topic:

Key vocabulary:

Outline of main ideas:

Notes/details/supporting examples:

Speaking Practice

Topic:

Key vocabulary:

Outline of main ideas:

Notes/details/supporting examples:

The following lists of selected vocabulary include a sampling of the types of vocabulary words that appear in these four MET practice tests and are provided here for study and review purposes. The words were taken from these practice tests, including the test items, listening scripts, and reading passages. All the words presented here are used in one or more of these practice tests, but this does not mean the words appear as test items, nor will they necessarily appear on an actual MET. In other words, this is not to be taken as a comprehensive vocabulary list, but rather a starting point to help with the preparation for these specific practice tests and follow-up review. Each of these vocabulary lists includes words likely to be used by language learners at the corresponding CEFR levels, but keep in mind that many words appear in more than one CEFR level, depending on the specific use or meaning. For this reason, the words are grouped into two sets (A2/B1 level words, and B2/C1 level words), based on the most common meanings and usage.

Selected Vocabulary: Practice Test 1

A2 to B1 Level Word Families

absent	contest	geography	quantity
accompany	continent	glove	rail
achieve	convince	goal	receipt
admit	cookie	greet	recipe
advance	cream	guitar	recycle
advise	create	gymnasium	refund
agent	crew	habit	register
album	damage	include	relax
ancient	defend	individual	repair
announce	defense	instrument	result
annoy	definite	intelligence	review
article	delay	interview	role
attempt	deposit	jazz	sandal
attitude	design	keyboard	score
avoid	detail	last	series
basket	direct	lecture	shade
belt	disabled	length	shampoo
bike	disappear	link	shave
biology	distance	literature	short
bite	dot	mail	signature
block	drum	match	smart
breathe	duty	medicine	soap
cafeteria	encourage	mineral	staff
cave	engage	mix	style
celebrate	entertain	modern	succeed
century	equip	newspaper	talent
ceremony	essential	opposite	topic
character	examine	original	traffic
charm	exercise	paragraph	transport
chess	exhibit	passenger	trumpet
chew	experiment	patient	twin
circle	fan	pollute	typical
common	fashion	pool	upper
compose	finance	print	variety
confidence	flight	prize	welcome
consist	frequent	puzzle	yoga
contact	future		

B2 to C1 Level Word Families

abstract	except	mixture	recruit
accomplish	factor	nominate	rehearse
ancestor	fake	notify	reject
appeal	firm	numerous	release
archaeology	gender	obtain	relieve
associate	harm	organic	remark
bark	icon	outcome	reproduce
candidate	impress	passion	reside
carbon	innovative	personality	risk
choir	insert	perspective	scholarship
claim	inspire	poison	skip
classic	institute	policy	soak
clue	investigate	practical	specific
collaborate	journey	predator	spirit
complex	launch	preserve	stereotype
conduct	legal	primary	stretch
critic	log	process	surge
debate	major	promote	tuition
digest	march	psychology	tune
discipline	mature	publish	ultimate
diverse	measure	rebel	undergo
emphasis	medical	recognize	volunteer
endure	minor		

Selected Vocabulary: Practice Test 2

A2 to B1 Level Word Families			
accident	direct	label	schedule
account	direction	library	search
active	disappoint	likely	season
alive	discuss	loose	secret
approve	display	luggage	sharp
attend	document	metal	silver
bicycle	due	minimum	similar
blame	efficient	monkey	sink
borrow	enemy	object	slice
brain	fail	operate	social
brand	false	opinion	solve
cancel	familiar	period	speed
career	foreign	piano	stream
casual	frame	pipe	teenage
chat	fuel	pleasure	temporary
chemistry	garage	poem	terrific
clinic	gift	politics	therefore
coast	graduate	popular	thief
coin	height	private	tip
colleague	hobby	profession	toast
concentrate	inch	property	tour
contain	increase	pure	trade
cousin	injure	regular	tube
culture	intend	repeat	tunnel
describe	international	request	union
destroy	interrupt	routine	urgent
diet	introduce	scene	value
dinosaur	journalist		

acid	dissolve	instruct	remove
affect	donate	interact	resolve
alter	dual	interfere	restrict
alternative	dump	interior	resume
amateur	economy	landlord	reveal
ambassador	element	loss	root
appropriate	emperor	majority	sale
aspect	empire	manufacture	satisfy
assign	erosion	military	seldom
assume	establish	miner	shell
assumption	evidence	minimal	simultaneous
automatic	exploit	mint	solid
balance	extend	mission	sophisticated
broadcast	extensive	mud	source
category	exterior	multiple	standard
chaotic	fame	network	submit
chill	fascinate	nutrition	substantial
circumstance	fault	oak	supervise
commerce	flexible	official	surface
community	formal	origin	symbol
complicate	fortune	panel	theft
conflict	fund	participant	threat
consequence	gap	participate	thrill
considerable	global	presence	thus
consume	hammer	prestige	tool
consumption	hazard	prior	trace
contribute	headquarters	priority	tradition
copper	helmet	proceed	tutor
corporate	host	produce	valid
debut	ideal	prove	vast
decade	illustrate	purchase	venue
deceive	image	regret	virtual
disorganized	inquire	reinforce	

Selected Vocabulary: Practice Test 3

A2 to B1 Level Word Families

advantage	contract	language	screen
annual	creature	league	separate
apology	custom	lively	shark
argue	cycle	method	sheet
attract	decision	monument	skill
audience	deliver	occasion	spare
author	disease	opportunity	spectacular
benefit	dozen	organize	stain
border	drama	photocopy	stir
broad	elementary	positive	stress
brochure	expert	product	surround
bunch	extreme	professor	switch
calm	festival	progress	technique
comment	firework	purpose	translate
communicate	ghost	quality	trash
conclusion	kitten	section	weak
adult	elephant	partner	soul
bowl	exam	path	stadium
calendar	fantastic	pink	storm
capital	furniture	poster	toy
competition	insect	prefer	umbrella
concert	map	president	uniform
correct	menu	receive	upset
crowd	negative		

B2 to C1 Level Word Families

absurd	demonstrate	internal	precise
accurate	detect	invite	pressure
acquire	determine	lesson	publication
administration	diplomat	linguistic	qualify
adopt	dissertation	litter	quiz
assist	distinguish	locate	recognize
bonus	distort	logic	reflect
budget	distribute	mammal	replace
campaign	edit	marathon	represent
campus	effective	memo	reputation
characteristic	emotion	merit	response
cherry	enable	modify	shelter
citizen	error	muscle	shift
client	evaluate	observe	signal
commit	expand	obstacle	slot
committee	facilitate	organ	steel
concept	feature	overview	task
confuse	flash	parade	texture
congratulate	gate	passage	theory
contrast	generate	perceive	tide
convey	highlight	personnel	transmit
correspond	hire	physical	underestimate
criticism	identify	picturesque	unite
cultivate	impact	plot	visual
decline	indicate	possess	wander
define	intense		

Selected Vocabulary: Practice Test 4

A2 to B1 Level Word Families

access	compete	industry	project
adventure	condition	ingredient	pump
advice	confirm	improve	questionnaire
alarm	connect	initial	rare
anxious	convenient	install	relative
apartment	copy	invent	remote
apply	crash	knowledge	rescue
architect	currency	laboratory	research
architecture	customer	limit	respect
atmosphere	demand	magazine	robot
attach	department	material	roof
attack	description	message	semester
attention	deserve	model	session
available	develop	navy	smooth
average	discount	nervous	soccer
background	effect	novel	society
balloon	electric	ocean	software
belong	energy	option	solution
boss	entrance	otherwise	speech
bounce	essay	pattern	sweater
branch	excellent	percent	technology
brief	exchange	perform	text
cable	explore	phrase	tiny
candy	file	physics	tongue
carpet	float	plastic	towel
challenge	generation	platform	update
chapter	grade	population	various
climate	guide	powder	warn
comparative	importance	previous	western
compare	independent	principal	

absorb	device	interpret	recommend
adjust	distinct	journal	recreation
alternate	disturb	lounge	refer
appetite	eagle	lung	regard
appoint	entire	maintain	regulate
assess	eliminate	manual	remain
atom	enterprise	mayor	resign
boost	environment	mechanism	resource
burst	eventually	moderate	retail
calculate	evolve	monitor	rural
cell	expense	motive	shallow
chemical	explosion	necessity	significant
cholesterol	expose	negotiate	species
combine	extract	oblige	strength
commute	focus	occur	strip
component	foundation	optimist	structure
conscious	frankly	overwhelm	substance
construct	function	oxygen	summary
consult	gasoline	ozone	survey
content	geology	philosophy	survive
context	harsh	potential	therapy
contradict	hesitate	pretend	thorough
craft	immediate	procedure	unique
crucial	incident	profit	upcoming
current	influence	propose	voluntary
deadline	insight	protein	weird
delicate	institute	rapid	worthwhile

Answer Keys

Practice Test 1

1.	A	26.	B	51.	D	76.	D
2.	B	27.	D	52.	C	77.	B
3.	C	28.	C	53.	B	78.	B
4.	B	29.	A	54.	C	79.	D
5.	C	30.	A	55.	B	80.	C
6.	B	31.	B	56.	C	81.	B
7.	B	32.	B	57.	D	82.	D
8.	D	33.	A	58.	D	83.	C
9.	A	34.	B	59.	B	84.	B
10.	B	35.	B	60.	B	85.	C
11.	D	36.	C	61.	A	86.	C
12.	D	37.	D	62.	D	87.	C
13.	B	38.	C	63.	A	88.	B
14.	A	39.	B	64.	C	89.	D
15.	B	40.	A	65.	D	90.	D
16.	C	41.	C	66.	B	91.	B
17.	B	42.	C	67.	D	92.	A
18.	B	43.	C	68.	A	93.	D
19.	A	44.	D	69.	C	94.	C
20.	A	45.	C	70.	C	95.	D
21.	B	46.	A	71.	D	96.	A
22.	B	47.	B	72.	A	97.	C
23.	B	48.	B	73.	C	98.	A
24.	B	49.	C	74.	B	99.	D
25.	C	50.	B	75.	A	100.	D

Answer Keys

Practice Test 2

1.	C	26.	D	51.	C	76.	B
2.	A	27.	B	52.	D	77.	D
3.	D	28.	C	53.	D	78.	C
4.	B	29.	A	54.	B	79.	D
5.	B	30.	D	55.	D	80.	B
6.	C	31.	D	56.	A	81.	C
7.	A	32.	B	57.	A	82.	A
8.	B	33.	C	58.	A	83.	A
9.	A	34.	A	59.	C	84.	B
10.	A	35.	C	60.	B	85.	A
11.	C	36.	C	61.	A	86.	C
12.	D	37.	C	62.	A	87.	C
13.	D	38.	A	63.	B	88.	A
14.	D	39.	D	64.	D	89.	D
15.	C	40.	D	65.	D	90.	C
16.	B	41.	D	66.	B	91.	B
17.	B	42.	B	67.	C	92.	B
18.	D	43.	B	68.	A	93.	B
19.	C	44.	A	69.	A	94.	A
20.	B	45.	B	70.	C	95.	A
21.	A	46.	A	71.	C	96.	A
22.	C	47.	A	72.	A	97.	B
23.	B	48.	B	73.	A	98.	D
24.	A	49.	B	74.	C	99.	A
25.	B	50.	A	75.	D	100.	C

Practice Test 3

1.	A	26.	D	51.	A	76.	B
2.	C	27.	A	52.	B	77.	A
3.	D	28.	D	53.	B	78.	C
4.	D	29.	B	54.	B	79.	C
5.	D	30.	D	55.	C	80.	A
6.	D	31.	C	56.	C	81.	D
7.	B	32.	A	57.	C	82.	D
8.	B	33.	B	58.	B	83.	A
9.	A	34.	A	59.	A	84.	D
10.	B	35.	D	60.	B	85.	B
11.	D	36.	D	61.	B	86.	D
12.	C	37.	C	62.	D	87.	C
13.	D	38.	A	63.	D	88.	A
14.	A	39.	A	64.	A	89.	B
15.	D	40.	A	65.	B	90.	A
16.	C	41.	C	66.	D	91.	C
17.	A	42.	B	67.	A	92.	D
18.	C	43.	A	68.	B	93.	B
19.	C	44.	A	69.	A	94.	D
20.	B	45.	B	70.	A	95.	B
21.	C	46.	D	71.	B	96.	B
22.	A	47.	D	72.	B	97.	D
23.	A	48.	A	73.	B	98.	D
24.	B	49.	B	74.	D	99.	B
25.	C	50.	D	75.	A	100.	A

Answer Keys

Practice Test 4

1.	A	26.	A	51.	A	76.	D
2.	A	27.	A	52.	A	77.	D
3.	D	28.	C	53.	D	78.	B
4.	B	29.	A	54.	B	79.	C
5.	C	30.	D	55.	C	80.	B
6.	C	31.	A	56.	D	81.	D
7.	D	32.	A	57.	A	82.	A
8.	A	33.	C	58.	D	83.	D
9.	D	34.	D	59.	B	84.	C
10.	B	35.	A	60.	C	85.	D
11.	B	36.	B	61.	D	86.	D
12.	C	37.	C	62.	A	87.	A
13.	A	38.	C	63.	C	88.	C
14.	C	39.	A	64.	B	89.	A
15.	C	40.	D	65.	D	90.	B
16.	D	41.	D	66.	D	91.	C
17.	A	42.	D	67.	B	92.	B
18.	B	43.	C	68.	C	93.	C
19.	C	44.	A	69.	C	94.	C
20.	D	45.	D	70.	B	95.	A
21.	D	46.	A	71.	D	96.	A
22.	C	47.	C	72.	B	97.	D
23.	C	48.	C	73.	D	98.	C
24.	C	49.	A	74.	B	99.	A
25.	B	50.	B	75.	A	100.	D

Practice Test 1
Listening, Part 1

1.

F: I just arrived on Flight 947 from Chicago, and my suitcase wasn't in the baggage claim area.

M: Several passengers on that flight had their luggage delayed because of tight connections. Let me check the system to confirm.... Can I see your baggage claim check, please?

F: Sure. Here it is.

M: OK. Yes, your luggage is coming on the next flight. Please fill out this form with your contact information, and we'll have it delivered to you.

N: What happened to the woman's luggage?

2.

M: I've been accepted to two universities, and I can't decide which one to choose.

F: That's great—which ones?

M: One is the University of Utah, and the other is Ohio State. They're both excellent schools, and their tuition fees are also about the same.

F: Hmm. Well, I don't know much about either institution, but, for what it's worth, the mountains in Utah are absolutely beautiful.

N: According to the woman, what might help the man decide?

3.

M: Can you let Jake know that the website is down again?

F: It is? Since when?

M: We're not sure, but it probably went out sometime yesterday.

F: Oh my! This isn't the first time it's happened. He's gotta get that fixed once and for all.

N: What are the speakers mainly discussing?

4.

F: Hey, why did you skip Science today? I thought it was your favorite.

M: It is, but our English teacher asked me to write a speech for this year's graduation ceremony, so I'm using class time for that.

F: Wow. And you're gonna sing in the choir, too?

M: Probably not. I need to focus on giving the speech.

N: Why did the man miss class?

5.

F: Do you know what the weather in Portugal's like in January?

M: It's similar to Spain because they're really close to one another. Why? Are you planning a trip?

F: Yeah, and I was wondering if I should pack sandals and a swimsuit.

M: You'd be better off with gloves and a hat.

N: What does the man suggest the woman do?

6.

F: May I help you?

M: Yes. I'd like to register for classes for the next semester. Here's my registration form.

F: Did you get your advisor's approval? I don't see a signature.

M: Oh. Sorry, I forgot to do that. I'll come back later then.

N: What problem does the man have?

7.

M: I have to say, Michelle, these cookies are absolutely delicious.

F: Oh, thanks. I'm glad you like them.

M: They're really good—some of the best I've ever had. You'll have to give me the recipe sometime.

N: What does the man want to do?

8.

M: How was your vacation in Paris? Did you have good weather?

F: It was perfection. If only I could've stayed!

M: Must be hard being back at work.

F: It's definitely taking some time to get used to again.

N: How does the woman feel about her trip to Paris?

9.

M: Excuse me. Could you tell me where I can find the shaving cream?

F: Sure. It's at the far end of Aisle 6, between the shampoo and vitamins.

M: Oh! Near the soap?

F: Exactly.

N: What does the man want to buy?

10.

F: Your plants look awful. Have you been watering them?

M: It's not lack of water. It's the sunlight.

F: What do you mean? They haven't been getting enough light?

M: Actually the opposite. I found out too late that these plants grow best in the shade.

N: What happened to the man's plants?

11.

M: You know, Monday is the deadline for professor-of-the-year nominations.

F: Right. And you want to nominate Professor Wilson, don't you?

M: Of course! She's the best professor I've ever had. And I know you also like her more than you're willing to admit. And I just need one other student to second my nomination.

F: Fine, fine. I'll do it.

N: How does the woman feel about the man's idea?

12.

M: Professor, I need some help understanding the passage you've assigned for next class.

F: You mean the one on cultural stereotypes?

M: Exactly. I don't understand what it means when it says, "There isn't a relationship between cultural characteristics and the traits of actual people."

F: It means that most stereotypes are based on generalizations and opinions, like saying that all young people are irresponsible.

N: Why does the student talk to the professor?

13.

M: You won't believe who got the marketing job at my office! Do you remember the tall guy I went to business school with?

F: You mean Tom? The smart, quiet guy? But I thought he was in London working for a European designer.

M: Well, he just got back, and he'll be working with me for the new campaign. Isn't that great?

N: Why is the man happy about the new employee?

14.

F: I found this same printer at one of your competitor's for 20 dollars less. See? Here's the advertisement from today's newspaper.

M: Ah. That's no problem. We'll be happy to match that price.

F: In that case, I'll take it.

M: Great. I'll have one of the cashiers ring it up.

N: What did the woman want?

15.

M: Excuse me, Professor, have you returned last week's papers? I didn't get mine back yet.

F: The assignment on American painters? You wrote on Georgia O'Keefe, right?

M: No, no. Remember, I asked if I could write about the Spanish painter Pablo Picasso instead?

F: Of course. That was really well researched.

N: What can be inferred about the professor?

16.

F: Now that we've finished interviewing everyone, we've got to make our decision. Did any of the candidates stand out to you?

M: To be honest, all of them were impressive.

F: I agree.

N: How do the speakers feel about the candidates?

17.

M: Hey, I see you've got a new haircut.

F: Oh, yeah, just yesterday. I was actually just going for a little trim, but as it turns out, I got a little more than I was expecting.

N: What does the woman say about her haircut?

18.

F: Wow! Is that your new bike?

M: Yeah, isn't it great? My friend Bob built it especially for me. He measured the length of my legs, my arms, and my back and put together a bike that fits my body perfectly.

F: Do you think he could build one for me?

M: Sure. I warn you, though. It's great, but I'll be paying for it for the next two years.

N: What does the man say about the bike?

19.

M: Have you seen the posting for the new business scholarship?

F: No. Are they giving full funding? Because I could really use it!

M: It's from a marketing firm that's offering to pay tuition fees in exchange for 20 hours of work per week. There's also the possibility of being hired full-time after graduation.

F: Sounds great! I'll definitely apply.

N: What is required of the student who gets the scholarship?

Listening, Part 2

Numbers 20 to 23.

N: Listen to a conversation in a gym.

M: Hello. I'm looking to join a gym in the area, so I'd like some information.

F: Sure, I'm glad to hear you're interested in joining us here at Frank's Fitness. We have two different plans available to new customers. The less expensive option is ... well, it's called the Basic Pass. You can use the weight machines, free weights, and the exercise machines, but you have to pay extra for classes. Then there's the Unlimited Pass, which gives you free access to all the classes, and it costs 75 dollars more than the Basic per month.

M: Hmm. That's tough. I really don't know. Usually I just prefer to exercise by myself—you know, lift weights.

F: The classes are a lot of fun. There's aerobics, yoga, karate—you name it. And we even have dance classes—salsa, tango, and a couple of other kinds too.

M: Huh. I've always wanted to learn to dance.

F: Well, how about this? You can try the Unlimited membership for a month, and if you decide you don't need the classes, then you can go down to the Basic for the second month.

M: That's not a bad idea. Let me give it some thought.

20. N: What are the speakers talking about?

21. N: What is the difference between the Basic Pass and the Unlimited Pass?

22. N: What will the man probably do?

23. N: Why does the woman say: And we even have dance classes—salsa, tango, and a couple of other kinds too.

Numbers 24 to 26.

N: Listen to a conversation between two friends.

F: John! John! I've been looking everywhere for you. Have you seen the notice on Professor Evans' door?

M: Did she post the grades for our research project? Or did she cancel our lab class again? I could use the extra time.

F: No, no. This has nothing to do with our class. There's a new science contest starting in two weeks. They're offering a prize to the team that comes up with the most innovative project. Do you want to enter with me?

M: Sounds exciting. I'd love to, but I'm taking so many classes. I'm really short on time as it is. Do you need a partner to join?

F: It's not necessary, but I could really use your help. You know a lot more about science than anyone else I know.

M: Maybe I could just help you come up with ideas. What's the contest about anyway?

F: That's the challenge. All the materials have to be recycled. Anything new is off limits. The idea is to find new uses for stuff people normally throw away.

M: Mmm. Now that's a great idea.

24. N: Why was the woman looking for the man?

25. N: What will the man most likely do?

26. N: What does the man mean when he says: I'm really short on time as it is.

Numbers 27 to 30.

N: Listen to a conversation between a publisher and a cookbook author.

F: I think we're almost ready to publish my cookbook. Yesterday I finished testing the new recipes and they're all in good shape.

M: I'm glad to hear that! Now, about the pictures of the main dishes....

F: Oh, yes, I've been meaning to ask you about that. When are we going to take the photographs?

M: Actually, I've got a new idea to discuss with you. I was thinking that maybe we could hire an artist to do some colorful drawings of your recipes instead of using photographs. It could even be that painter friend of yours I met last week. It would add an interesting artistic touch to the book, and it will most likely lower the price of printing.

F: Hmm, I never thought about that…. That sounds a bit different for a cookbook though.

M: Yeah, but that's exactly what I'm going for. It could be taken as a really novel idea, which may be a good marketing strategy.

F: Well, if you think so, I guess it's worth a try.

M: Great! So I'll contact your friend.

27. N: What are the speakers mainly discussing?

28. N: What did the woman think of the new recipes?

29. N: Why does the man mention the woman's friend?

30. N: What does the woman mean when she says: I guess it's worth a try.

Numbers 31 to 33.

N: Listen to a conversation about some research.

M: I think the research you've done is really interesting. Would you spend a little time explaining the chart that you included with your study?

F: Sure, no problem. Okay, now as you know, Introduction to Geography is a requirement for geography majors. Of course, other students can also take it, but it's a required class for the major, and it's a prerequisite for all upper-level geography classes, so most majors take it in either their first or second year.

M: Right. Got you so far.

F: OK, so, what I did was compare the average grades for geography majors who take it in their first year versus majors who take it in their second year.

M: Oh, I see. I thought these were two different courses.

F: No, no, it's the same course. I just wanted to see whether second-year students did better in it. And, it looks like they do.

M: Yes. Now that I understand what you did, I can see that. They seem to do a lot better. That's interesting. Why do you suppose that is?

F: Well, I think it's because second-year students bring more background knowledge into the classroom. But, not only that. They're just better students all around. They have more classes under their belts and have figured out how to be more effective students in general. They have better study habits, that sort of thing. And, of course, they're just more mature. They're a little more serious than first-year students.

31. N: What does the woman say about the course?

32. N: How does the woman explain the results of her study?

33. N: What does the man mean when he says: Right. Got you so far.

Listening, Part 3

Numbers 34 to 37.

N: Listen to an announcement by a public official.

F: Today marks the historic opening of Preston City's new electric railway. For the first time ever, public transportation will connect the city center to the suburbs. This will help thousands of citizens save money and cut their daily travel time by up to 30 minutes. Plus there will be many other advantages. These new trains will reduce traffic congestion, create new jobs, and reduce pollution. We all have the Chester Rail Company to thank for getting the project done so quickly. Although there were some setbacks, ultimately the delay was short, and the project was completed within only a few months of the original timeline. I'd also like to thank local residents for your patience during the road closings and construction delays of the past years. I think you'll find the result well worth it.

I do have to ask for your continued patience for the next few weeks though. Construction crews are still finishing up in the area of Logan Street, so there may be some minor delays. If you'd like to know how the delays may affect your travel, you can look at the PrestonCityRailway.com website for daily updates. Working together with all our city's residents, I look forward to continuing to improve our fine city for years to come. Thank you very much.

34. N: Why does the speaker mention creating jobs and reducing pollution?

35. N: Why does the speaker thank the local residents?

36. N: Why does the speaker suggest looking at the website?

37. Listen to a part of the talk again. Then answer the question. Although there were some setbacks, ultimately the delay was short, and the project was completed within only a few months of the original timeline. N: What does the speaker mean when she says: Although there were some setbacks.

Numbers 38 to 41.

N: Listen to a manager talking to her staff.

F: As you know, five new people are starting in our group on March tenth. They'll meet with Human Resources that morning, fill out paperwork, go over corporate policies. Then they'll be brought here, to their offices, where the tech staff will show them the ropes: learning how to log in, navigate email, timesheets, and so on. By then, they might be feeling pretty overwhelmed. You remember your first day here—filling out that paperwork, learning your way around this huge building, trying to remember everyone's names—and I thought, instead of confusing them by having a big welcome lunch, we'd have each of them go with just one person from the group. So, on that first day, five of you will be assigned to someone to take to lunch in the company cafeteria. I'll send out an email today to those of you who will be on "lunch duty." I'd also like to ask the rest of you to help make the new people feel welcome. Invite them for a quick coffee break, and stop by their offices occasionally to see if they have any questions. Now I know that most of you are flying to Boston tomorrow for the conference and are really busy getting ready for that, so I'll let you all get back to work now. Do stop by if you have any questions though.

38. N: How does the speaker think the new employees will feel?

39. N: What does the speaker want some staff to do?

40. N: What will the staff probably do next?

41. N: Listen to a part of the talk again. Then answer the question. Then they'll be brought here, to their offices, where the tech staff will show them the ropes: learning how to log in, navigate email, timesheets, and so on. N: What does the speaker say about the tech staff?

Numbers 42 to 46.

N: Listen to a professor speaking to a music class.

M: I know that some of you hope to find jobs as directors of concert bands, and one of the things you'll need to do as a band leader is to select the music—that is, the songs—to include in each concert your band plays. Of course, a director should keep the tastes of the audience in mind, but it's also important to consider the musicians themselves—that is, what type of music will keep band members interested? So, there are two main concerns: difficulty and diversity.

First, you should select pieces that include a range of difficulty levels. Some songs should be fairly easy to play and others should be more challenging. However, it's important to make sure that even the more challenging pieces are not beyond the musician's level of ability. Remember: the harder the music is, the more the musicians will have to practice. Once, I was directing a community band, and there was a really complex trumpet part. The trouble was, during practice, the other band members had to wait while the trumpets played their part of the music over and over until it sounded right. Before I knew it, there were only five minutes of rehearsal left! So you have to remind musicians to practice the more difficult parts at home.

Another thing to remember is variety: include pieces that vary in both style and pace. A variety of music will appeal to all musicians. Some prefer classical music; some prefer more modern music. You want to include something that appeals to band members' varied tastes.

Let's practice this, OK? I'd like you to work with a small group and make a list of songs that a high school band might play for a concert, keeping in mind the information we've just covered.

Audioscripts

42. N: What is the professor mainly discussing?

43. N: Why does the professor mention trumpet players?

44. N: What advice is given about challenging music?

45. N: What will the students do next?

46. N: What does the professor mean when he says: A variety of music will appeal to all musicians.

Numbers 47 to 50.

N: Listen to part of a radio report about a book.

F: Today I want to talk about a fascinating book that I just read. It's called *The Runner in You*. It's about the writer, Jerry Hampton, a guy who started running about fifteen years ago. But he kept getting injured. Then one day he came across a magazine article about the Tarahumara tribe in Mexico—a group of people who regularly run 50-mile races for fun … in handmade sandals. He was amazed and decided to do some investigating. He soon learned that the Tarahumara runners were not suffering from the kinds of foot problems that people who wear expensive shoes to "protect" their bodies were—that is, people like himself who wear special shoes to protect their feet from the effects of running. So Hampton decided to start running barefoot. He's now run two marathons without suffering from any of the injuries that bothered him when he wore expensive running shoes. So his hypothesis is that the shoes are causing the problems, that the natural structure of our feet and bodies enables us to run long distances without harm. This makes sense to me. I've suffered a lot of running injuries myself over the years, all while wearing expensive shoes. But I must say, Mr. Hampton is not a doctor. In the book he's clear about his lack of medical credentials. But I think that some real scientists will do some experiments soon, and in the meantime he's advocating that everyone start running barefoot.

47. N: What is the main point of Jerry Hampton's book?

48. N: What does Jerry Hampton have in common with other runners?

49. N: What does the woman think will happen in the future?

50. N: What does the speaker mean when she says: In the book he's clear about his lack of medical credentials.

Practice Test 2
Listening, Part 1

1.

M: Good afternoon. Can I help you find anything today?

F: Hi, yes. I was wondering if you have this shirt in a different color. I need to buy something for my cousin, and he prefers bright colors.

M: Yes, we have other colors on the rack in the back of the store, but they aren't on sale.

F: Oh, I'm not worried about that. I'll go take a look.

N: What does the woman want to do?

2.

F: Enjoying the conference, Tim? Wasn't the welcome dinner great last night?

M: Definitely, and the keynote speaker was terrific, but I'm disappointed in the way the rest of the conference is turning out. Don't you find things to be a little...chaotic?

F: Well, now that you mention it. The scheduling could be better.

M: Better?! Nearly half the workshops have been cancelled or their locations are changed at the last minute!

N: Why is the man disappointed?

3.

F: I think if this semester ends as planned, I'll be graduating in the summer. How about you?

M: I'd wanted to finish this year, but I haven't fulfilled the science requirements yet.

F: Can't you take classes during the summer and graduate in the fall?

M: No, I'm going home to help my dad with his business.

N: What will the man do in the summer?

4.

F: And what can I get you, sir?

M: I'll just have a hot chocolate.

F: OK. And what kind of milk do you want that made with?

M: Oh, what kind of milk? Oh, umm, uh, just regular milk, I guess.

N: Why did the man repeat the woman's question?

5.

F: Can you get this package to corporate headquarters today?

M: Sorry. You just missed the last pick-up, and the courier won't be making another trip till tomorrow morning.

F: Okay, well, this is extremely high priority, so I'll drive it up there myself this afternoon.

N: Why will the woman go to corporate headquarters?

6.

F: Hi, Steve. How's school going?

M: I'll sure be glad when this semester's over—that's all I can say.

F: Really? That rough, huh?

M: Yeah. I'm taking more classes than I can handle. I've never worked harder in my life.

N: What problem does the man have?

7.

M: I see you bought a new car. It's quite a bit smaller than the old one though.

F: I know, but that big car was costing me a fortune on gas. This time I decided I'd buy the most fuel-efficient car I could find.

N: What is true about the woman's new car?

8.

M: What do you think of Professor Miller's article in the chemistry journal this month? His new research project sounds fascinating!

F: You know, I haven't even opened this month's journal. I'm about to start grading my students' final papers, but reading his article is at the top of my list of things to do as soon as I get a chance to take a break from all this work.

N: What will the woman do next?

9.

F: Excuse me, but how much are those tall bookcases?

M: The oak ones? Those are 180 dollars each.

F: Oh, I'm on a student budget. Do you have something, um, a little more reasonable?

M: We do have something similar in pine.

N: How do the bookcases compare?

10.

F: Well, my professor gave me back my paper, and I have to do it all over again.

M: Wow! And you worked so hard on it.

F: It's my own fault. He gave us detailed instructions but....

M: But you never read them? Hey, I've been there myself. We all have.

N: What happened to the woman?

11.

F: So, how do you like your new job? I hear it's quite different from anything you've done before.

M: Well, it's growing on me. This career change was more a financial necessity than a personal choice, but I'm enjoying the new routine more than I'd expected.

N: What does the man say about his job?

12.

F: How was your party? Did you get some nice gifts?

M: Well, I got some clothes, some books, and a set of luggage.

F: I thought you were getting a new computer.

M: That's what I wanted.

N: How does the man feel?

13.

F: David, do you know when the history final is?

M: I forget the exact date, but I think the test is sometime after our presentations.

F: Really? I thought it was the week before.

M: Well, I have an appointment with the professor tomorrow. I can double-check with her then.

N: What will the man ask the professor?

14.

M: Have you looked at the resumes we've received for the computer programmer position?

F: Yes, but only a few of the applicants have hands-on work experience.

M: Well, I don't want to rule someone out because of that alone. Familiarity with new programs is what's essential. The field is changing rapidly, and a recent graduate could very likely know more about new technology than someone who graduated ten years ago.

N: What does the man think is required for the job?

15.

M: Are you ready for your trip yet?

F: Just about. I still need to pick up a map and pull out some warm clothes. The guidebook says it's chilly in Paris this time of year.

M: It can be, but whatever you do, make sure you bring good shoes. You'll be doing lots of walking.

F: Yeah, I know. I'm looking forward to it though.

N: What is the woman planning to do?

16.

M: I'm looking forward to Jane's presentation tonight about virtual social networks.

F: Could be interesting.

M: Yeah. She's focusing on the way the internet is changing how people interact with each other.

F: I really like some of the new sites that people from all over the world are using to meet each other. I hope she has something positive to say and doesn't just deal with security concerns.

N: What will the presentation be on?

17.

F: Can I help you?

M: Uh, yes, I'd like to open a bank account.

F: Oh, no problem. Please have a seat, and I'll get Mr. Miller, our account specialist, to explain our various options and help you decide what's going to work best for you.

M: OK, thanks.

N: What will probably happen next?

18.

F: Bill, I have a first-year student who needs a math tutor. Would you be interested in helping her?

M: I'm pretty busy this semester, but I might be able to do it.

F: Well, think it over. Maybe it would be good to talk to her about it. I've got her information here somewhere.

M: OK. I'll think it over and give her a call.

N: What will the woman do next?

Audioscripts

19.

M: Oh, man, my weekend was terrible! A pipe broke under my kitchen sink. Water got everywhere! My apartment's a total mess!

F: Oh, no! That's awful!

M: The landlord said I have to move out temporarily while the repairs and clean up are being done.

F: My brother might have room, if you need a place.

N: What does the man need to do?

Listening, Part 2

Numbers 20 to 23.

N: Listen to a conversation in a store.

F: May I help you?

M: Yes, thanks. I was wondering if this pair of shoes is on sale. There's a sale sign hanging over part of the display table, so I'm not sure which shoes on the table are on sale.

F: Uh. I've had at least ten customers ask me about this. We'll have to fix the display. Only the shoes that are under the sale sign are being discounted this week. Not the ones on the left side of the table.

M: Oh, that's too bad. I really like this pair, but they're so expensive.

F: Yeah, it's a good brand. Did you see the black shoes that are on sale? They're a lot less pricey.

M: Oh, I did. Those are too casual though. I need something suitable for a business trip.

F: Well, if you want, you can try the dressier pair on. And if you really like the way they fit, I can ask the manager if he'd give you a special discount. The store's good about trying to make customers happy. Want to give them a try?

M: Sure, thanks.

20. N: What is the store's problem?

21. N: Which shoes are on sale?

22. N: What did the woman offer to ask the manager?

23. N: What does the woman mean when she says: They're a lot less pricey.

Numbers 24 to 26.

N: Listen to a conversation in a university office for international students.

F: Welcome to the International Center. How can I help you?

M: I saw a flyer for the International Student Welcome Party, and I'd like to sign up, please.

F: Wonderful! You just need to write down your name and student identification number here. The welcome party is this Saturday at 7 o'clock. It'll be held in the university's West Meeting Hall, right next to the Student Union. It should be a nice opportunity to meet other international students. How long have you been with us here on campus?

M: I've been in the country since summer, but I just came to campus at the beginning of this semester, a little less than a month ago. I've had a good time so far, but I'd definitely like to meet some new people. It can be difficult to make friends when you're in a brand-new place.

F: Yes, that's why we host this social event every semester. The party will begin with some introductions and fun activities to break the ice. Then we'll serve food and give everyone a chance to chat and get to know each other. Later in the night, there'll be music and games.

M: Sounds great. I'll look forward to it.

24. N: Why does the man visit the office?

25. N: How does the man feel about his time at the university?

26. N: What does the woman mean when she says: The party will begin with some introductions and fun activities to break the ice.

Numbers 27 to 30.

N: Listen to a conversation between a business owner and a customer.

M: Good morning. What can I get you today?

F: I'll just have a large coffee, please, with room for cream.

M: Okay. That'll be $1.50.

F: Sure. Say, the noise from the construction out there must be driving you crazy. I work around the block, and it's been bothering us. But to have it going on right in front of you....

M: Yeah, it's pretty bad. But that's not the worst of it. They've been working on the street all week, as you know, but starting Monday, they're gonna rip up the sidewalk as well. It's gonna be almost impossible for people to get into the cafe.

F: Wow. And for how long will that be?

M: Only a week, they tell me. But a week of business is a week of business. But...what are you gonna do?

F: I know. Well, I'm sorry to hear that. But you'll still see me coming in for my morning coffee next week.

27. N: What are the speakers mainly talking about?

28. N: Why is the man upset?

29. N: What is probably true about the woman's coffee drinking?

30. N: What does the man mean when he says: But...what are you gonna do?

Numbers 31 to 33.

N: Listen to a conversation between a professor and a student.

M: Hi, Professor. I was wondering if we could talk about Saturday.

F: Yes, certainly. I think you're gonna enjoy it. I could tell from the paper you wrote that you really got a lot out of reading the play, and I know that once you actually see it performed, you'll get an even deeper understanding, and there....

M: Well, that's just it, Professor. It doesn't look like I'm gonna be able to make it.

F: Really? Why?

M: It's my job. I've talked to my supervisor, and I've tried to find someone to take my shift, but I'm not having any luck. My supervisor says I should've told him a month ago.

F: I'm really sorry to hear that. We were only able to get the discount on the tickets because I waited till the last minute, but I guess that leads to other problems.

M: But this isn't going to count against me, right? You said that attendance wasn't mandatory.

F: No, no, don't worry about that. It's not. It's just a shame that you'll miss out on a production that's said to be quite good.

31. N: What problem does the student have?

32. N: Why did the professor wait to buy the tickets?

33. N: Listen to part of the conversation again. Then answer the question. F: You'll get an even deeper understanding, and there.... M: Well, that's just it, Professor.... N: Why did the student interrupt the professor?

Audioscripts

Listening, Part 3

Numbers 34 to 37.

N: Listen to part of a lecture in a biology class.

F: Yesterday, we started discussing the possibility that some animals are aware of numbers and may even be able to count. So, what's needed to be able to count? At a minimum, it requires the ability to see that objects are in the same group or category—that they have a sameness.

Next, you need to name things in some way. Humans might use, for example, words like *first, second*, and *third*, but it's not really necessary to use numbers or words. This is an important point that we'll come back to in tomorrow's lecture when we discuss animal behavior, especially in regard to categorizing, in more detail.

Okay, so, counting requires identifying sameness and a labeling system, but it also requires keeping track of what's been counted, and what hasn't.

Now, before discussing true counting in animals, let's consider a more basic behavior: being able to distinguish between a small number and a large number, making a comparison—keeping in mind that being able to compare is not the same as counting. Now, several studies have shown that monkeys can tell the difference between a set of, say, five objects and a set of ten objects. But they have a harder time distinguishing between a set of ten and a set of eight. In other words, the ratio, or the magnitude of the difference between the sets, is important. Interestingly, humans and monkeys are similar in this regard—when the difference between two sets is small, it's harder to make a distinction.

34. N: What is the talk mainly about?
35. N: What will the professor probably discuss in the next lecture?
36. N: What does the professor say about distinguishing small numbers from large numbers?
37. N: What does the professor mean when she says: the magnitude of the difference between the sets is important.

Numbers 38 to 41.

N: Listen to a talk by a police officer.

M: Good morning, everyone. I'd like to thank the director of Hilltop Community Center for inviting me to come here today to talk about one of the most common problems in our city at the moment—that's bicycle theft. Every year thousands of bicycles are stolen, and I'd like to talk about a few ways to avoid anyone taking your bicycle.

Right, first of all you need to know that about half of all bicycles are taken from people's own property. So, when you leave your bike at home, put it out of sight in a secure place—in a garage or something like that—and keep the door locked. When you have to leave your bike somewhere that is not your own property, choose the location carefully. Avoid isolated or dark places, and try to find somewhere many other people leave their bicycles too.

You also need to be careful about what you lock your bike to. You should always lock your bike to an immovable object: a bike rack or ground anchor. If possible, lock both the wheels and the frame of your bike to the object. That way, no one will be able to take any part of your bike. Don't forget to secure or remove articles that can be taken off your bike—for example, a speedometer, lights, or even a pump. Anything that's not locked is easy for a thief to take, and that's exactly what we want to avoid.

38. N: What is the speaker mainly discussing?
39. N: Why does the speaker mention garages?

40. N: What does the speaker state about locking a bicycle?

41. N: According to the speaker, what should bike users do in addition to locking their bikes?

Numbers 42 to 46.

N: Listen to a lecture at a conference.

F: Good afternoon everyone. It's a pleasure to be at the third annual Children's Health conference. My talk today will focus on a study my colleagues and I have done showing that children are increasing their consumption of beverages sweetened with sugar and that this has consequences for their health.

The number of calories children get from sugary beverages has increased over the past two decades in the United States. We looked at both younger children and teenagers and found that they are currently getting about twenty more calories a day from these beverages than children did twenty years ago. This may not sound like much, but it's actually a substantial increase in calories. You should consider that these drinks are very low in vitamins and other nutrients. This means children are adding empty calories, or calories that offer little health benefit, to their diet. We found that sugar-sweetened beverages make up about 16 percent of the total number of calories most teenagers consume daily. To put this into perspective, a teenage boy would need to spend over three hours walking to be able to burn off these extra calories.

The bottom line is: children are taking in more calories than they're burning—they're getting more than they need. The result is that kids are gaining weight. We feel that reducing the consumption of sugary beverages would benefit kids' health and help them keep fit.

42. N: What is the speaker's main purpose?

43. N: What does the study show about children's diet twenty years ago?

44. N: Why does the speaker mention "empty calories"?

45. N: What did the study find is true about many teens in the United States?

46. N: What does the speaker mean when she says: This may not sound like much, but it's actually a substantial increase in calories.

Numbers 47 to 50.

N: Listen to a director speaking to a group of employees.

F: Hi, everyone. Thanks for making time for our staff meeting today. I've heard there are still quite a few questions about the new vacation policy, so I thought it might be best if we could go over it together.

Under the previous policy, everyone automatically got ten days off a year of paid vacation time, plus four paid national holidays. The new policy may seem more complicated, but in the end, might actually work out better for you.

You see, with the new policy, all employees still get four paid national holidays, but the amount of paid vacation time you get depends on how long you've been with the company. After your first two months on the job here—that is, after you complete the training and probationary period—after your first two months, you'll accrue one vacation day for each month you work. So, the first year you're here, you'll earn 10 days off, but in the years after that, you'll earn 12 days off each year—that is, one day per month—and that's more vacation than the previous policy allowed.

Also, a note about using your vacation time: you should notify your supervisor at least one week before you want to take time off. We try to accommodate everyone's requests, but we can't have too many people out at the same time.

I know this is a lot to process, so please, if you have any questions, do feel free to contact me.

47. N: Why is the woman speaking to the employees?

48. N: Why does the woman think that employees will approve of the vacation policy?

49. N: What must an employee do in order to take time off?

50. N: What does the speaker mean when she says: We try to accommodate everyone's requests, but we can't have too many people out at the same time.

Practice Test 3
Listening, Part 1

1.

M: OK, class. Now that we've reviewed the article, take about ten minutes to write down a few of the most important points the author makes.

F: Um, how much should we write?

M: Oh, three or four sentences will do. Just highlight the main ideas.

N: What are the students supposed to do?

2.

F: Hey, Matthew! Remember that pet shelter that I told you about last week?

M: The one for animals who need homes? Sure.

F: Well, I went back last night, and I adopted three kittens.

M: You did what?!

N: What does the man think about what the woman said?

3.

M: Hey, Pat, I wanted to talk to you about your final project.

F: Sure. What is it?

M: Since you have such a strong interest in Asian literature, maybe you can incorporate the works of some modern Asian writers in your report.

F: Thanks, Professor. That's a great suggestion. I'll think about how I can do that.

N: What does the professor recommend the student do?

4.

F: Are you going to the game tonight?

M: I was hoping to go. What time does it start?

F: The stadium gates open at 5, and the game starts at 6. But if you're driving, you should get there really early. The parking lots fill up fast.

M: That's what I heard. I definitely need parking.

N: Why should the man go early?

5.

F: Did you read Frank's predictions for sales for the coming year?

M: Yeah, I did. I'm not sure what to say.

F: Well, I'd say they're off the wall! I can only hope that he hasn't sent them to the finance committee yet.

N: What does the woman think about Frank's predictions?

6.

F: You really could use another bookcase.

M: I know. All of these stacks of books and papers are starting to look a little messy—even to me.

F: I'm sure you could get one really cheap. People are always having moving-away sales around here.

N: What are the speakers mainly discussing?

7.

F: I heard that the midterm's gonna be really hard.

M: Yeah, me too. Professor Morrison has a reputation for giving tough tests. Maybe we should meet up at the library sometime this week and study together.

F: That's a good idea. Having a study partner helps a lot; we can, you know, explain things to each other and quiz each other. It's way better than studying alone. When's good for you?

M: I'm done with classes by 1 every day, so any time after that works for me.

N: What will the speakers probably do next?

8.

M: How many people do you need to go with you to San Diego next week?

F: At least one other person to help with everything—and, because it's our first time there, a technology person as well.

M: You don't think IT will be able to help you over the telephone?

F: We'll be setting up 30 laptop computers. If something goes wrong, telephone calls or emails won't be enough.

N: How does the woman feel about the trip to San Diego?

9.

M: Welcome to City Hall. You'll need to sign in and show ID before going upstairs.

F: Sure. This is actually my first time here. Where do I go to get a business license?

M: The licensing office is on the second floor.

F: Thank you.

N: What is the woman planning to do?

10.

M: I'm looking for a bowling league to join. Can you tell me what days there are leagues available?

F: Yeah. We have men's leagues on Mondays and Thursdays and women's leagues on Tuesdays and Fridays. Wednesday nights are our mixed leagues.

M: That last one sounds great. Can I sign up for it?

F: OK. Here's the application. Fill this out, and we'll find you a team.

N: Which league did the man ask to join?

11.

M: Why is the campus so crowded this weekend?

F: It's Alumni Weekend.

M: Ah, that explains why I just saw a bunch of 40-year-olds wandering around on the Quad.

F: Yup, once a year they all come back to relive their college days.

N: What are the speakers commenting on?

12.

F: A group of us are thinking about going to the basketball game on Saturday. Wanna join us?

M: To be honest, I'd rather watch paint dry.

F: OK—just thought I'd ask!

N: What does the man think about going to the basketball game?

13.

M: There was an email today about the meeting on Tuesday. Do we have everything we need?

F: I think so. I collected all the memos, and I'll bring them to the meeting so everyone can review them together.

M: Sounds good.

N: What will the woman do on Tuesday?

14.

M: Hey, where'd my chair go? I was only gone a minute.

F: Sorry, I didn't notice; I was busy studying. You know, it seems like there are more people than seats in the library these days, so I'm not surprised.

M: Yeah, it's every man for himself around here.

N: What does the woman say about the library?

15.

F: I signed up for the 5K race this weekend, but something came up. Could you cross me off the list?

M: Sure. What is your name?

F: Ann Jones.

M: OK. You're all taken care of.

N: Why did the woman mention a list?

16.

M: How is your lab experiment going?

F: I don't have the precise results yet, but so far it looks like they support my theory.

M: That's good. So you'll be able to start writing your dissertation soon?

F: That's right.

N: What does the woman say about her experiment?

17.

M: The list of John's merits is clearly very long, but before we go into that, maybe we should talk about any concerns that we have about him.

F: I don't really have any—except that he's so well qualified for the position that we might have trouble keeping him for long.

N: What do the speakers agree about?

18.

M: Can this new photocopier really do everything that the old one could?

F: That's a good question. It's less than half the size.

M: Yeah. And taking a quick look at the menu, it doesn't look like it can staple.

F: I don't understand the logic of replacing a copier with a new one that does less.

N: How do the speakers feel about the new photocopier?

19.

F: Good morning, Bill. Do you have any idea why it's so dark in the office?

M: I'm afraid the electricity is out. It probably happened during the storm last night. We're waiting for the electric company to come now.

F: I hope we won't have to wait too long.

N: Why is the office dark?

Listening, Part 2

Numbers 20 to 23.

N: Listen to a conversation in a university.

F: Professor Bradley, I need some advice about choosing a major.

M: Didn't we talk about this last semester? I thought you were set on studying history.

F: That's true, but then I started thinking that a history degree might not be useful in today's job market. Business administration also interests me, and the skills are in high demand, so now I'm debating between the two.

M: Well, your decision really depends on what type of work you want to do and when. If you want to get a full-time job right after graduating, then you will probably have more options available to you with a business degree. But if you're still thinking about becoming a professor, then by all means stick with history.

F: What about a double major? I could study both.

M: That's another option, although that will be a lot more work.

F: I've got a lot of thinking to do.

20. N: What is the woman trying to do?

21. N: What does the man say the woman should consider?

22. N: How does the woman feel about her decision?

23. N: What does the man mean when he says: I thought you were set on studying history.

Numbers 24 to 26.

N: Listen to a conversation at a doctor's office.

F: OK, Mr. Jefferson, that'll be 25 dollars for the visit today, and would you like to go ahead and schedule your next appointment?

M: Sure, I guess. But when do I need to come back? My flu seems to have cleared up. I feel fine now.

F: We recommend at least one visit a year, even if you're in good health. And that's what's typically covered by insurance. But if you're feeling unwell, or develop some health concerns, we urge you to call us and we'll get you in ASAP.

M: Got it.

F: So how about I schedule you for two o'clock on Thursday, October eighth of next year. That's just about a year from today.

M: I don't have my calendar with me, but that'll probably be OK. If not, can I call and change it?

F: It's pretty easy for us to change appointments that far off into the future. But it can be a problem if it's more immediate. That said, we do leave some appointment slots open for people who are ill to be able to make a last-minute appointment. Like I said, don't be afraid to give us a call if you need to come in before that.

M: OK. Thanks.

24. N: What are the speakers mainly discussing?

25. N: What will the man probably do later?

26. N: What does the woman say might be a problem?

Numbers 27 to 30.

N: Listen to a conversation between coworkers.

F: Thanks so much for coming with me to the warehouse, Sam. I'm not sure I could have loaded these boxes of books into the van by myself.

M: No problem. It really would have been difficult for one person to lift them. Glad I could help.

F: So, these are all going to our new bookstore on Forty-Second Street. I was hoping we could drive to the store right away and bring them inside, but since it's raining so heavily now, that's probably not a good idea.

M: Yeah, I think you're right. It would be terrible if the books got water damage.

F: OK. Why don't we just park the van at the store, but not unload anything until the rain subsides? There are plenty of other things we can do at the store while we wait.

M: That sounds like a good idea. Is the new store still scheduled to open next Monday?

F: Yes—that's the plan, but it isn't set in stone. We may have to push the opening date back a few days.

27. N: What does the woman want the man to help with?

28. N: What is implied about some boxes?

29. N: Why will the speakers wait to complete a task?

30. N: What does the woman mean when she says: Yes—that's the plan, but it isn't set in stone.

Numbers 31 to 33.

N: Listen to a conversation between two students.

M: So, Kristin, you're off to London for graduate school in August, right? Sounds exciting! Are you ready? Have you figured out your housing situation?

F: Funny you should ask. That's the only thing I haven't figured out yet. I have a place on campus for the first month, but it's not available for the full year.

M: That sounds stressful. Do you know anyone in London who can help you?

F: I actually don't know a soul in London. But there's a graduate housing office that I've been in contact with. They've been really helpful sending me details on all the different options that are available.

M: But none of them look good enough to commit to?

F: Well, that's just it. The internet is fantastic—to a certain point. I just don't want to commit to something until I actually see it in person—the room and the surrounding area. But I do have a few areas in mind, and I'll be checking them out the first week I'm there.

M: Well, sounds like you're on top of things. I'm sure it'll all work out.

F: Hope so!

31. N: What are the speakers mainly discussing?

32. N: How does the man feel about the woman's preparations?

33. N: What does the woman mean when she says: I actually don't know a soul in London.

Audioscripts

Listening, Part 3

Numbers 34 to 37.

N: Listen to a talk in a psychology class. The professor is talking about a research study.

M: Today, we're going to discuss a research study about the brain. It's really shed some light on how we perceive color. In the study, researchers had infants and adults look for a flash of light in the shape of a circle. They had to visually locate the light as it flashed against a similarly colored background. Sometimes the light appeared on the right side of their field of vision. This side of vision transmits to the left side of the brain, the part where language is processed. Sometimes the light appeared on the left side of the field of vision. The left side of vision connects to the right side of the brain, the side that is pre-linguistic. This side does not use language to process information.

Researchers tracked the infants' eye movements and found they did better when the light appeared on their left side. Adults did better when the light appeared on their right side. This suggests that the way adults see color is connected to their use of language. And that babies see colors with the non-linguistic part of their brains. When and how this change occurs, and just what these differences mean, is still unknown. But the study shows that babies and adults process color differently.

The difference may be related to language acquisition. This hypothesis is supported by what we already know about language and color: that various languages categorize and define colors differently. For example, Russian speakers define shades of blue that English speakers see as a single color.

34. N: What is the research study about?
35. N: What did the people in the research study do?
36. N: Why does the professor mention Russian speakers?
37. N: What does the professor mean when she says: It's really shed some light on how we perceive color.

Numbers 38 to 41.

N: Listen to part of a lecture in a creative writing class.

F: As we start the next lesson, I want to read something to you, and it may sound familiar: "You are standing in front of two doors. The one on the left is made of steel. The one on the right is made of wood. If you choose the left door, turn to page 93. If you choose the right door, turn to page 112."

I expect that some of you might be familiar with this type of story. It's called a "Choose Your Own Adventure" story.

Choose Your Own Adventure stories are children's books that first appeared in the 1970s. What made these stories unique was that they were written in the second person, and this made the reader the main character, who had choices that could lead the path to different places in the story. In other words, a reader could read the same book several times and the story would be different each time. By the middle of the 1980s, these stories were among the most popular selling children's literature in the United States. Yet, as the saying goes, what goes up, must come down. By the middle of the 1990s, the popularity of these stories had declined.

Today, Choose Your Own Adventure stories are increasing in popularity once again, as parents who remember the stories from their childhood introduce these books to their children.

38. N: What is the talk mainly about?

39. N: Why does the speaker read to the class?

40. N: What is special about the stories described in the talk?

41. N: What does the professor mean when she says: Yet, as the saying goes, what goes up, must come down.

Numbers 42 to 46.

N: Listen to a presentation at a local company.

M: Good afternoon. I've got great news to announce. DNJ Marketing has finally signed a contract to acquire Bradshire Advertising. As of today, the two companies have officially merged, but we'll keep the name DNJ Marketing. Don't worry; there won't be any lay-offs. In fact, this is an opportunity for DNJ to expand. We plan to hire fifty new employees over the coming year.

Our goal is to combine the two companies in a way that takes advantage of our strengths and resources. To this end, we've created a Transition Task Force to guide us through this time of change. The task force, led by Larry Johnson, Bradshire's former Vice President of Human Resources, is made up of personnel from both companies. The task force will coordinate the reorganization of our departments. There are many details to work out, but we know that the company headquarters will remain here in New York. The only big shift is that all production and publication operations will be moved to Bradshire's old headquarters in Texas. Although it won't be mandatory, there'll be incentives for some employees from both companies to relocate to the different offices.

I'd also like to take this opportunity to thank Margaret Lomax for her role in making this merger happen. As Assistant Director of Finance, she worked closely with Bradshire for over a year on this important deal. It's my pleasure to announce her promotion today to Vice President of Finance. She'll also be a key member of the Transition Task Force. Congratulations, Margaret! Thank you for your hard work.

42. N: What is the speaker's main purpose?

43. N: Which of the following will most likely be a duty of the Transition Task Force?

44. N: What major change for DNJ Marketing does the speaker mention?

45. N: Why was Margaret Lomax promoted?

46. N: Why does the speaker say: To this end, we've created a Transition Task Force to guide us through this time of change.

Numbers 47 to 50.

N: Listen to a speaker talking to a group of community volunteers.

M: Thanks, everyone, for coming. I'm really happy that there's such a great turnout for this event. Thank you all for sparing time to help clean up our community and raise awareness about the problems with plastic bottles.

So you've all probably noticed how many discarded plastic bottles there are littering the area. Today we're going to do our best to pick up as many as possible. So one group—Team 1—will be going to parks and walking along busy sidewalks, et cetera, to pick up litter. Then were going to separate out the plastic bottles, glass bottles, and aluminum cans, you know, to see to it that they get recycled.

The other team—Team 2—is going to work on distributing materials for our latest public awareness campaign. We've produced brochures and posters explaining the environmental impact of all these plastic bottles, and what's more, the fact that plastic bottles are not only bad for the environment, but also bad for us. Recent research shows that dangerous chemicals can leak from the plastic into drinks. So, were trying to promote the use of reusable stainless steel drinking bottles. Hopefully, this will result in less trash and better health.

OK, so let's go ahead and team up, and get started. Team 1, you can pick up bags at the table near the door. Team 2, the promotional materials are right here with me. And, I've got maps for both teams. Let me know if you have any questions.

47. N: What is the speaker mainly discussing?
48. N: What is the speaker's goal?
49. N: What does the speaker imply about stainless steel drinking bottles?
50: N: Listen to a part of the talk again. Then answer the question. Then we're going to separate out the plastic bottles, glass bottles, and aluminum cans, you know, to see to it that they get recycled. N: What does the man mean when he says: to see to it that they get recycled.

Practice Test 4
Listening, Part 1

1.

F: I'm looking for the textbook for my physics course, but you're all out of the one I need. Could you order a copy for me?

M: Sure. That usually takes about five business days, unless I have it sent by express mail, but that's gonna cost you an extra ten dollars.

F: No problem! Class starts next week.

N: What will the woman probably do?

2.

F: Do you happen to know the Dollar-to-Euro exchange rate?

M: I'm not sure. Why do you ask?

F: Well, I want to order a sweater from this catalog, but the prices are all in Euros.

M: Try looking online. There're plenty of websites that do currency conversions.

N: What problem does the woman have?

3.

F: Were you able to get tickets for the concert?

M: I wish! All the cheap tickets were sold out by the time I got to the box office. The tickets they had left were too expensive.

F: That's too bad. I know you were looking forward to going.

M: I was. Oh well. I just waited too long, I guess.

N: How does the man feel?

4.

M: Um, Professor? I was absent from class on Monday. I was wondering if I could get a copy of the handouts from the lecture.

F: Of course. I'll be in my office today from noon until four; drop by anytime to pick them up.

M: Did I miss a lot?

F: Well, we covered most of what's in chapter six in your textbook, so you'll want to go over that carefully.

N: Why did the man talk to the professor?

5.

F: Are you okay, Steve? You look a little tired.

M: I am tired, very tired. I came in early for a conference call with the London branch. They could only meet in the morning there, and because of the time difference, that meant I had to be here at 4 a.m.

F: No wonder you're tired! You should go home early then.

M: I think I'm going to go home at about 1.

N: What will the man probably do?

Audioscripts

6.

F: I'm terrible about paying bills on time. This is the second month in a row I've had to pay a late fee because I mailed my cable payment in late.

M: You know, you can set up a lot of your bills so that the payments are deducted automatically from your bank account. I do that for all my utilities, and my cell phone as well. It's really convenient, and I don't have to worry about late payments anymore.

F: That's a good idea. I never thought about that before.

N: What does the man suggest the woman do?

7.

F: I'm so nervous about meeting with the dean tomorrow.

M: Oh, right! You're the new student government representative. Aren't you requesting money for the sports club?

F: Actually, I proposed a new program to improve freshman students' experiences. The dean liked it and asked us to expand the plan.

M: How about offering new students a campus tour? That map they give is hard to read.

N: Why is the woman meeting the dean?

8.

M: Taylor Office Supply has raised their prices again, almost ten percent on most of their stuff. And that's the second price increase this year. I'm afraid it's time to find a new supplier.

F: I've heard OfficePro has good prices, although their selection is a bit limited. But they might be good for ordering basic, everyday supplies. Should I have them send a catalog?

M: Yes, that'd be great.

N: What will the woman probably do?

9.

M: How was that new movie you went to see yesterday?

F: You know, it's really funny. When we got there, all the shows were sold out, so we ended up getting tickets for later today.

M: Wow. I didn't realize it would be so popular.

F: We didn't either.

N: What can be inferred about the woman?

10.

F: I've been having quite a time trying to land a job. I've been looking for weeks. There's just nothing in my field listed in the newspapers.

M: Do you belong to any professional organizations? They can be a great resource for their members.

F: Actually, I do belong to the Teacher's Society. I don't know why it didn't occur to me to look into that.

N: How has the man helped the woman?

11.

M: How much was that management course that you took last weekend? I'm thinking about taking it myself.

F: It was just under a hundred dollars, and I think it was worth it.

M: Does that cover everything? Would I need to purchase books or software?

F: Yeah, the fee includes everything: two full days of instruction and a workbook with a CD that has all the lecture notes, examples, and practice exercises.

N: What does the man want to know?

12.

F: I like your new glasses. They really suit you.

M: Thank you. And I can see a lot better with them—especially when I'm reading. But it's weird. There's a blurry, unfocused spot on the left lens.

F: It doesn't look like they're dirty or anything—sounds like something's wrong. I'd take them back if I were you—have them make you a new pair.

N: What does the woman suggest the man do?

13.

F: Have you heard anything from John about his new job?

M: Yes, he says it's a long commute, but he really likes what he's doing.

F: That's good to hear. I know he was nervous about changing jobs. He told me it paid quite well, but he wasn't sure he'd actually enjoy the work.

M: Well, it seems to have worked out for him.

N: What was John's concern?

14.

F: Tony, I'm starting to get concerned about your class participation. Just showing up isn't enough. You need to get involved in the discussions.

M: But I do all the course readings and papers.

F: I know, but you still need to contribute in class. Your classmates have never heard your thoughts on the topics. That's as important as doing well on the exams.

N: Why did the woman talk to the man?

15.

M: Have you heard the news? The mayor just resigned from office.

F: Do you know who's gonna take over?

M: I hope it's someone with the same qualifications because he was excellent.

N: What does the woman want to know?

16.

M: John told me you're taking a course in web design at the community college. Are you doing that for work or ...?

F: For work mostly. My boss wants an internal website for our department, and I thought this would be a good opportunity to learn some new skills, plus the company's paying for the class.

N: What will the woman probably do?

17.

F: How's selling your house going? Did that couple who was so interested make an offer to buy it?

M: Actually they did, but it fell through. After three weeks of negotiating, we couldn't agree on a couple points, so they decided not to buy it. So it's back to square one.

F: Don't worry. It'll all work out.

N: Why is the man upset?

18.

M: Hi, Katie! How's your training going? Your big bike race is only two weeks away, right?

F: I'm pretty sure I'll be ready. I've been riding a lot—every day after work—and, uh, taking long rides on the weekends. But, I'm not racing to win, just to finish.

M: Like a personal goal?

F: Exactly. I just want to prove to myself that I can do it.

N: What are the woman's expectations for the race?

19.

F: Here are the first-quarter sales figures you asked for.

M: Thanks. Do I need to double-check them? Or do you feel confident that they're accurate?

F: Well, Joan put them together, and Bill looked them over. And they're the two most meticulous people we have.

N: What does the woman say about the figures?

Listening, Part 2

Numbers 20 to 23.

N: Listen to a conversation about an apartment.

M: Hi, I'm Steve Walters. I called earlier about seeing the apartment.

F: Oh hi, Steve. I'm Nancy. Come on in. Uh, sorry for the mess, I'm in the middle of packing everything up, as you can probably tell by all the boxes.

M: Oh, no problem. Wow! This place is a lot bigger than I imagined! Most of the apartments I've looked at in this neighborhood are really small.

F: Yes, this is unusually large for the area.

M: And this is a great location—near the subway, the grocery store. Wow, and look at all the light you get in here! Those big windows! The last place I looked at today was like a cave—really small, tiny windows, no light. Um, so, how much is the rent again?

F: It's 800 a month, but that includes gas, electricity, and trash collection. But you will have to pay for water, but that never cost me more than another twenty dollars a month.

M: That's a very good deal. Um, and uh, when would the apartment be available?

F: On the first. As you can see, I'm still in the process of packing, but I'll have all my stuff moved out of here on the twenty-eighth or twenty-ninth. I hired a professional cleaning service to come in and scrub everything and to shampoo the carpets, and all that kind of stuff. It'll be like new when they're done, and ready for a new tenant to move in on the first. Well, uh ... come on, I'll give you a tour of the rest of the place.

20. N: Why is the man visiting the woman?

21. N: What does the man describe as a cave?

22. N: What is NOT included in the monthly rent?

23. N: According to the woman, what will happen soon?

Numbers 24 to 26.

N: Listen to a conversation between a student and a professor.

F: Hello, Professor, may I come in?

M: Of course. What can I do for you?

F: Well, the final's in two weeks. I was wondering if you might have a list of topics to study, or ... old tests we could look at? I want to make sure I'm thoroughly prepared.

M: I haven't prepared anything specific. And the old tests wouldn't help because the course content changes from year to year.

F: Hmm. What do you suggest I do?

M: Well, in a nutshell, you've got to be familiar with everything we've covered this semester. Go over the syllabus first. Make sure you're comfortable with all the topics on it. Then, if you find something you feel less confident about, go back to the textbook and handouts and whatever notes you took.

F: I've pretty much done that, but there's so much. I was hoping to get a more specific idea about what to focus on. We've covered a lot of material this semester, and I guess I'm not sure what's really important and what's, you know, not.

M: Sorry, but I can't help you any more than this.

24. N: What is the student discussing with the professor?

25. N: What does the professor say about the course content?

26. N: What does the professor suggest that the student do?

Numbers 27 to 30.

N: Listen to a conversation between two friends.

F: So, did you ever buy a laptop computer?

M: No, I'm still shopping around. It's a bit confusing. There're so many choices, and there's so much to read about. I want to make sure I get what I need, but I don't want to pay too much either.

F: You do have a lot to think about. Mind if I offer some advice?

M: No, that'd be great.

F: Whatever computer you get, buy an extended service warranty. You know, when you pay an extra fee and the computer is warrantied for, like, five years? Then, if something goes wrong and you need to get the laptop fixed or replaced—and believe me, eventually something will go wrong—you're covered.

M: That's a good idea. I hadn't thought about that.

F: I got one when I bought my laptop. I hesitated about it at first, but then a year later, when my hard drive failed, they replaced it for free. Turns out the cost of the warranty was way cheaper than buying a new hard drive.

M: Well, now you've given me another thing to look into.

27. N: What does the woman recommend that the man do?

28. N: What happened to the woman's computer?

29. N: How does the man feel about buying a computer?

30. N: Listen to part of the conversation again. Then answer the question. Then, if something goes wrong and you need to get the laptop fixed or replaced—and believe me, eventually something will go wrong—you're covered. N: What does the woman mean when she says: you're covered.

Audioscripts

Numbers 31 to 33.

N: Listen to a conversation between coworkers.

F: So, Stuart's retiring at the end of October. What are we going to do about replacing him?

M: I guess we need to start interviewing candidates as soon as possible.

F: Yes, I think we should get someone on board before Stuart retires. That way, Stuart can help with training his replacement. There's a lot to learn, and having some overlap with him will make things easier.

M: I agree. We want to have as smooth a transition as possible.

F: So, should I put a Help Wanted ad in the newspaper?

M: Yes, and we should probably post a notice on the Careers page of our website.

F: Yes, definitely. I'll go talk to Mary in Human Resources and ask her how to go about doing all this. I'm sure there's some procedure we need to follow.

M: I'm sure there is. Oh, when you talk to Mary, ask her for a copy of Stuart's job description. I'd like to sit down with him and update that. His position has evolved a lot over the last year, and I'd like to get all his current duties and responsibilities down on paper. In fact, maybe we should do that first—before we post the ad. We need to be clear in our own minds just what it is we're expecting from candidates.

31. N: What are the speakers talking about?

32. N: Why will the woman talk to Human Resources?

33. N: What does the man say he wants to do?

Listening, Part 3

Numbers 34 to 37.

N: Listen to a researcher giving a presentation to his colleagues. He is talking about a research study.

M: I want to share with you a study we did on how teens use the internet to find out about music. We interviewed over 1800 teens to ask them about their internet use, especially how they use the internet with regard to music. We spoke to all these young people face-to-face.

What we learned is that teenage girls are more likely than boys to use the internet to research a musician or a band. Girls are also more likely to go online to listen to music and watch music videos. About the only music-related activity that boys seem to do more of is downloading music to copy to CDs.

Another interesting thing we found is that teenage girls who spend a significant amount of time online—uh, about half of them spend at least a hundred dollars a year on buying music, buying music from online retailers—these girls actually prefer to get their music this way, rather than going to the store.

In our study, we also identified those teens who are the so-called "music influencers"—the ones who other people turn to for advice or opinions about music, the ones who seem to know what's new or cool in music. Music influencers also tend to be teenage girls. And these girls spend nearly a third more money on music than average teens, which makes sense: they're influencers because they listen to more music. They tend to have a wide range of musical tastes. And because they're spending so much time listening to music, they wind up buying more music.

34. N: What was the research study about?

35. N: How was the information for the study collected?

36. N: What does the speaker say about teenage girls who spend a lot of time online?

37. N: What kind of people tend to be music influencers?

Numbers 38 to 41.

N: Listen to a manager talking to her staff.

F: Good morning, everyone, and thanks for coming. I know there'll be some questions about the new ID cards, so I thought it'd be best to meet and discuss the changes as a group. OK, so I'll just jump right in. As of next month, we'll be using a new computerized system to keep track of employee hours. The system is tied into the ID cards you'll all be getting next Monday. So be sure to stop by the security desk on Monday morning to pick up your card. OK, so here's how it works. Your ID card'll have a magnetic strip on the back. We've installed card readers outside the building entrance. When you arrive for your shift, you'll need to swipe your ID card in the reader. This'll do two things. First, it'll unlock the door to the building so you can enter; second, it'll log the date and time that you arrived. This arrival time is what'll be used to calculate your hours for payroll. You're counted as being "at work" from the moment you enter the building. Now, when you leave at the end of your shift—or if for any other reason you need to leave the building—you need to swipe your card again. So, just to make sure we're on the same page: You need to log in with your ID card at the start of your shift, and you need to log out whenever you leave the building. OK, now, I see you have some questions. Please feel free to go ahead and ask right now.

38. N: What will the ID cards be used for?

39. N: When will the employees swipe their cards?

40. N: After the talk was finished, what did the speaker expect the audience to do?

41. N: Why does the woman say: So, just to make sure we're on the same page.

Numbers 42 to 46.

N: Listen to a tour guide in the city of Chicago.

F: Good morning, and welcome to the Architecture Tour of Chicago. On today's tour we'll visit some of Chicago's oldest buildings. We'll also introduce you to one distinct architectural style that shaped the city in its early days.

Before we begin our tour, I want to give you some background information. Many of you know that Chicago suffered a great fire in 1871, and that's quite important when considering the architecture. The history of Chicago's buildings can be divided into two parts—before and after the Great Fire. Chicago's a relatively young city: the first buildings were erected in the early 1800s. By 1871, the city contained more than 50,000 buildings, roughly 17,000 of which were destroyed in the fire. This meant much of the city had to be rebuilt. Today, though, we'll visit some of the older buildings in the city—ones that survived the Great Fire.

Many of the older buildings—like those we'll see today—are in a style called Italianate. Italianate was an architectural style that drew its inspiration from Italian villas. They have tall first floor windows, which allow the beauty of the interior to be shown off. One of the most defining features of Italianate-style buildings is their low-pitched roofs. I'll explain more about those later. You'll also have the chance to go inside two of the homes we see today, to experience close up the unique style. I do hope you've all brought your cameras along.

Audioscripts

42. N: What is the speaker's main purpose?

43. N: What is the main focus of the tour?

44. N: Why does the speaker mention Chicago's Great Fire?

45. N: According to the speaker, what will the people do on the tour?

46. N: What does the speaker mean when she says: One of the most defining features of Italianate-style buildings is their low-pitched roofs.

Numbers 47 through 50.

N: Listen to a professor speaking to her philosophy class.

F: We've got just a few minutes before class ends, and I want to let you know about a public lecture that's scheduled for tonight in Dodge Hall. The lecture is on "Climate Change and Ethics: What Do We Know and What Should We Do?" We'll be turning our attention to ethics in a few weeks, so I'm hoping if you attend this lecture—it is optional—that it'll whet your appetite for the subject.

Dr. Stephen Willis, a professor from Central University, will be the speaker. He's a theoretical meteorologist, an expert on computer simulations of the atmosphere and—and this is where he really diverges from most other climatologists—he's published articles in major philosophical journals.

It says here in the flyer that "Dr. Willis will summarize key scientific findings" and "he'll examine policy options and their ethical implications"—that is, what we should do about them.

I believe he'll be discussing the question of inter-generational fairness—fairness between generations. It's an interesting idea. We're used to thinking about ethics in terms of the here and now and dealing with questions about the relations between living beings. But one of the questions Dr. Willis is going to ask is whether those of us who are living today have ethical obligations to those who will inherit the earth hundreds of years from now. Most philosophers believe—and I concur—that we do, and frankly, based on the work he's done, I'd be surprised if Dr. Willis thought otherwise.

47. N: What is the speaker's main purpose?

48. N: Why does the speaker think the event will interest the students?

49. N: What does the speaker say about future generations of human beings?

50. N: What can be inferred about the speaker and Dr. Willis?

Writing Test Responses Commentary
for Practice Test 1

CEFR Level: A2

Task 1:

1. **Do you like meeting new people? How often do you meet new people?**

   Yes, i like. Twice a month.

2. **Where is a good place to meet new people?**

   Partys and school it's best place to meet new peoples.

3. **Tell us about an interesting person that you met.**

   Last month i meet my friend Alfonso, He is very funny and nice.

Commentary:

✓	✗
• The response minimally completes the task. • The connection of ideas is partially successful.	• Most sentences contain grammar errors ("Yes I like," "meet new peoples"). • Mostly simple vocabulary is used with no attempt at sophisticated words. • There is little control of punctuation and capitalization. • Few connective devices are used.

CEFR Level: A2

Task 2:

Some people believe workers should have to retire, or stop working, at a certain age. Other people believe older people's experience can help a company. Do you think there should be a required retirement age? Explain, giving specific reasons for your choice.

When People get older they get inable to do some works, so i think, when someone get elder He can retire if he want, but the company can ask some types because the person have lot of esperience in this area.

If someone Don't retire, the person starts to have a lot of physical and mental problems because his age don't aloud to so many things so the person start to get business

Commentary:

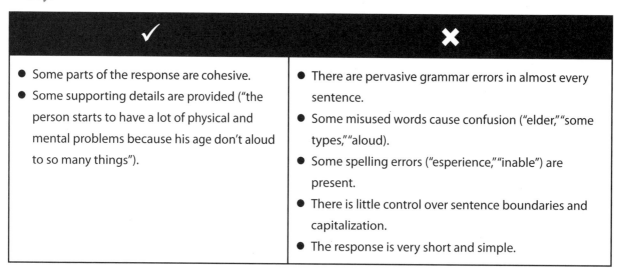

✓	✗
• Some parts of the response are cohesive. • Some supporting details are provided ("the person starts to have a lot of physical and mental problems because his age don't aloud to so many things").	• There are pervasive grammar errors in almost every sentence. • Some misused words cause confusion ("elder," "some types," "aloud). • Some spelling errors ("esperience," "inable") are present. • There is little control over sentence boundaries and capitalization. • The response is very short and simple.

CEFR Level: B1

Task 1:

1. **Do you like meeting new people? How often do you meet new people?**

   Yes, I really like meet new people, because you learn about society, how to treat with people you don't know and hang out more. I always meet new people.

2. **Where is a good place to meet new people?**

   I think that the best place to meet new people is a park or the internet, because in the park you can do a lot of activities, like playing soccer, for example.

3. **Tell us about an interesting person that you met.**

   I think that I don't have an Interesting person, or maybe yes. But im not good to identificate those people.

Commentary:

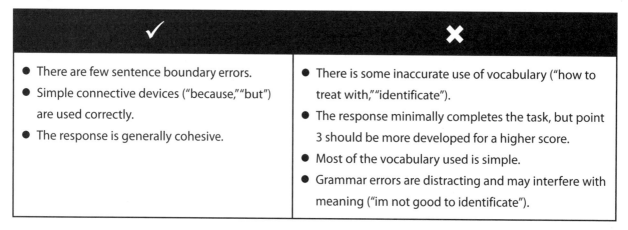

✓	✗
• There are few sentence boundary errors. • Simple connective devices ("because," "but") are used correctly. • The response is generally cohesive.	• There is some inaccurate use of vocabulary ("how to treat with," "identificate"). • The response minimally completes the task, but point 3 should be more developed for a higher score. • Most of the vocabulary used is simple. • Grammar errors are distracting and may interfere with meaning ("im not good to identificate").

CEFR Level: B1

Task 2:

Some people believe workers should have to retire, or stop working, at a certain age. Other people believe older people's experience can help a company. Do you think there should be a required retirement age? Explain, giving specific reasons for your choice.

I think that the person will decide if he wants or he can retire, but i also think that should be a Required Retirement age, like 55 years old, 60, 65, depending the job, for example if you Retire as an officinist, the Required Retirement age will be like 60 years old because at that age the most of the people dont Read very well.

But if your work is so hard like fireman, I think that the Required retirement age will be 50 years old and even less, because the firemans have to run, drive fast and well take a heavy ladder and save people in the house building, school, or other structure that is on Fire.

So in general I think that yes, there should be a Required Retirement age and that age is 50-55 years old. Now, Respect with the age and experience, I think that the older people In harvest jobs can "upgrade a level of his job" to Start working on a administrative type of work, for example, if he work as a fireman, he can leave his job to answer 9-11 calls. That's my opinion about this theme.

Commentary:

• The response is relevant and adequately completes the task (people with administrative jobs should have a later retirement age, those with more physically demanding jobs should retire earlier). • Some supporting details are provided. • Some simple constructions have no grammatical errors.	• Some misuses of vocabulary ("officist," "harvest jobs") occur. • Some parts of the response are cohesive, but others are difficult for the reader to follow. • There are frequent sentence boundary errors. • Most complex sentences contain errors. • Some repetition is present, which limits the text.

Writing Test Responses Commentary

CEFR Level: B2

Task 1:

1. Do you like meeting new people? How often do you meet new people?

No, I don't like meeting new people I meet new people once a month, in the street, in a party, etc.

2. Where is a good place to meet new people?

I think a good place to meet new people is a park or some after-school activities

3. Tell us about an interesting person that you met.

I met him in football. He knows a lot about football and it's so funny and interesting talk with him. Also, he has a lot of friends, and that makes me more talkative. Now, I'm not as shy as before I met him

Commentary:

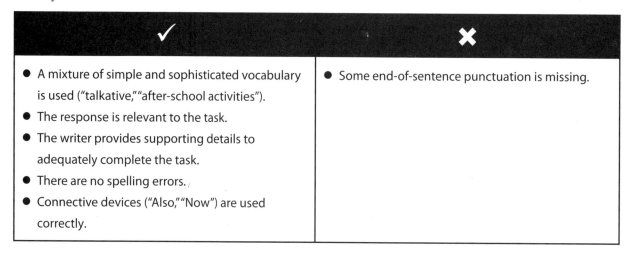

✓	✗
• A mixture of simple and sophisticated vocabulary is used ("talkative," "after-school activities"). • The response is relevant to the task. • The writer provides supporting details to adequately complete the task. • There are no spelling errors. • Connective devices ("Also," "Now") are used correctly.	• Some end-of-sentence punctuation is missing.

CEFR Level: B2

Task 2:

Some people believe workers should have to retire, or stop working, at a certain age. Other people believe older people's experience can help a company. Do you think there should be a required retirement age? Explain, giving specific reasons for your choice.

I think a required retirement age is a thing subjective. It's depend on the person and the job he/she have

For example, if you are a lawyer, it's more convenient to have old people near because, in general, they know a lot, they are more calm and with all their experience, they can give you more advices than a young lawyer. But some times, old workers are not as interesting as young workers, you can't talk about the same topics

In other jobs, like those that needs more movement, it's not convenient having old people there. For example, in a police station, older workers maybe have less habilities because they have less agility or energy tan youngers.

Taking both reasons, have a required retirement age is not good. The worker is who has to take the decision, not his/her around. Maybe his/her job is so important and retire bring him/her a lot of consequences, like a boring life or in a worse case, a depression, even if he/she has a family

Commentary:

• Some sophisticated vocabulary ("subjective," "convenient") is used. • The response is directly relevant to the task and explores both sides of the issue (retirement age in office jobs versus jobs that require physical activity).	• There are some grammar errors ("those that needs more movement"), but these do not interfere with meaning. • Some end-of-sentence punctuation is missing. • Some supporting details are provided but are not developed enough. • There are some errors with sentence boundaries in longer sentences (see paragraph 2).

CEFR Level: C1

Task 1:

1. **Do you like meeting new people? How often do you meet new people?**

   I do enjoy meeting new people, though I don't get to acquaint myself with such people as after as I would've liked. I meet new sets of people every few months whether its at an event or at one of the companies I get to visit.

2. **Where is a good place to meet new people?**

   Social events such as parties or maybe competitions are good places to meet new people, a few examples of competitions would be World Scholars Cup, or maybe Model United Nations since they have an atmosphere that puts you in the mood to talk, and there will be many different people to talk to

3. **Tell us about an interesting person that you met.**

   I once met a person named Matthew, and we got along pretty well He was a very smart kid, and he was full of never ending energy and enthusiasm. He was really interested in Quantum Physics and he could lecture you about for hours. He was also quite athletic, he used to do gymnastics and he was quite a fast runner.

Commentary:

✓	✗
• Errors are rare, even in complex sentences. • Sophisticated vocabulary is used ("got along," "never ending," "lecture," "puts you in the mood"). • The connection of ideas is always clear and successful. • The supporting details provided are well-developed. • The response fully completes the task.	• Some errors with sentence boundaries in long sentences occur, but these do not distract from the message.

CEFR Level: C1

Task 2:

Some people believe workers should have to retire, or stop working, at a certain age. Other people believe older people's experience can help a company. Do you think there should be a required retirement age? Explain, giving specific reasons for your choice.

There is a reason as to why retirement is a thing, and I personally think that whether or not or when a person retires is mostly up to them, but there may be exceptions.

As people get older, the state of their health generally gets worse. The elderly, for example, have problems with walking, hearing, seeing, talking and many other actions as well due to the fact that their health is not as great as it used to be. They start losing their cognitive abilities, as well as their physical abilities. This is the general rule, but there are exceptions. There are people who have managed to live over 100 years, yet they can still run and swim and do other mental activities near perfectly, and there are bound to be others like that, thought they may be younger. If such people are forced to retire, then that means lots of potential is being wasted, and it would be beneficial to the company if that person were to stay at his post or possibly be given an easier job, so as to minimize the chances of the employee making a mistake and causing a problem, which is likely to happen if the employee was facing cognitive or physical malfunctions due to their health being affected by age.

So the choice to retire should be up to the employees since they may still be in perfect shape for their current job, or they may still be fit for a simpler job, such as teachin or passing on his/ her knowledge and wisdom via lectures. There shouldn't be a "required retirement age," when somebody retires should be dependent on the person.

Commentary:

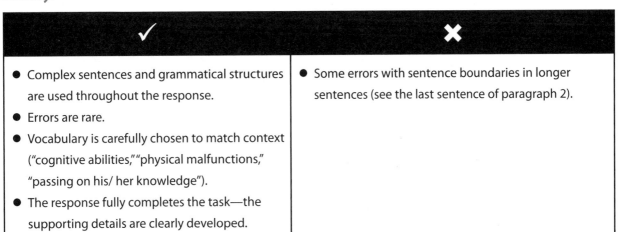

✓	✗
<ul><li>Complex sentences and grammatical structures are used throughout the response.</li><li>Errors are rare.</li><li>Vocabulary is carefully chosen to match context ("cognitive abilities," "physical malfunctions," "passing on his/ her knowledge").</li><li>The response fully completes the task—the supporting details are clearly developed.</li></ul>	<ul><li>Some errors with sentence boundaries in longer sentences (see the last sentence of paragraph 2).</li></ul>

Writing Test Responses Commentary for Practice Test 2

CEFR Level: A2

Task 1:

1. **Do you like to take photographs? What do you take photographs of?**

   Yes I do I take to my family

2. **Describe a place where you like to take photographs.**

   Yes I like, is to take photographs is phonie.

3. **Tell us about a photograph you took recently.**

   Photograph took recently is a happy birthday on my sister.

Commentary:

✓	✗
• Some basic thoughts are presented.	• Grammar mistakes create confusion for the reader. • Only simple vocabulary is used. • The response is short.

CEFR Level: A2

Task 2:

Some public places have a lot of garbage. One solution is to provide more trash cans for people to use. Another option is to increase penalties for people who throw garbage on the street. What do you think should be done? Use specific examples to support your opinion.

The places is good because, the garbage is terrible in the city, the people diven't have control, not importan in the floor garbage. Solution the problem garbage is: the person introduction have a conferment for a concietiser an contaminer of the city, the river and another person, because, produse the virus, take a ticket, and clean comunitari for 15th days. Use the gabechee for the garbage an use the bag. I done take a concienst the not garbage because and contamineret the mund, contamineiret the river, the family, the aire and the live, I take conscientizer and when you see another person for a garbage.

Commentary:

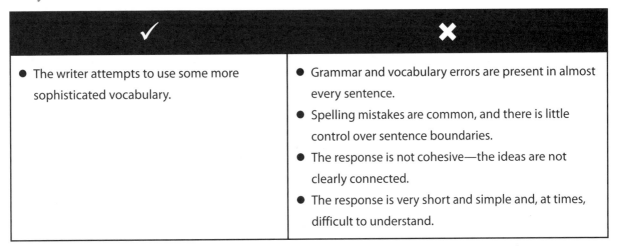

✓	✗
• The writer attempts to use some more sophisticated vocabulary.	• Grammar and vocabulary errors are present in almost every sentence. • Spelling mistakes are common, and there is little control over sentence boundaries. • The response is not cohesive—the ideas are not clearly connected. • The response is very short and simple and, at times, difficult to understand.

CEFR Level: B1

Task 1:

1. **Do you like to take photographs? What do you take photographs of?**

   Yes, I would like take photographs and, something that I think will be nice to take photos are diferents people and they culture.

2. **Describe a place where you like to take photographs.**

   I think Africa, India and Japan are good places to take this tipe of photographs but the culture are really special and signif.

3. **Tell us about a photograph you took recently.**

   A photograph that I took recently was sunset when the sky was realy beautiful and colorful.

Commentary:

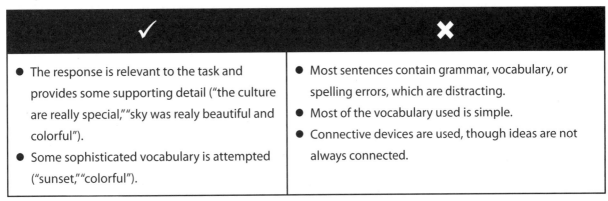

✓	✗
• The response is relevant to the task and provides some supporting detail ("the culture are really special," "sky was realy beautiful and colorful"). • Some sophisticated vocabulary is attempted ("sunset," "colorful").	• Most sentences contain grammar, vocabulary, or spelling errors, which are distracting. • Most of the vocabulary used is simple. • Connective devices are used, though ideas are not always connected.

Writing Test Responses Commentary

CEFR Level: B1

Task 2:

> Some public places have a lot of garbage. One solution is to provide more trash cans for people to use. Another option is to increase penalties for people who throw garbage on the street. What do you think should be done? Use specific examples to support your opinion.

At there days the garbage becomes a big problem because the public places and the streets were full of it. I understand that it looks like nothing but when we think on hoge quantity it becames the reason of lot of desasters like floods and the start of some epidemy.

To start, we could not dell on this topic without important and we should talk about it on the schools, on the companys, on the hospitals on the TV with helps of something interesting for the population pay attention. Another solution was creat programs that incentyvorts the treatment correct for the trash where has places specifying to separate and transformer it on oder stufs.

first when the people understand the important of they will started to they care of it.

Commentary:

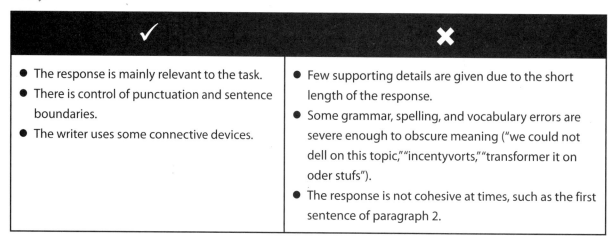

✓	✗
• The response is mainly relevant to the task. • There is control of punctuation and sentence boundaries. • The writer uses some connective devices.	• Few supporting details are given due to the short length of the response. • Some grammar, spelling, and vocabulary errors are severe enough to obscure meaning ("we could not dell on this topic," "incentyvorts," "transformer it on oder stufs"). • The response is not cohesive at times, such as the first sentence of paragraph 2.

CEFR Level: B2

Task 1:

1. **Do you like to take photographs? What do you take photographs of?**

   Yes I do. I love take phtographs so I take photographs of everything. For example, of landscapes, of myself, of my friends, of foods like, my meals and of me and my frends.

2. **Describe a place where you like to take photographs.**

   A place that I like to take photographs is outside. The illumination is better and more high quality.

3. **Tell us about a photograph you took recently.**

   The last photograph I took was of me and my friends in a party.

Commentary:

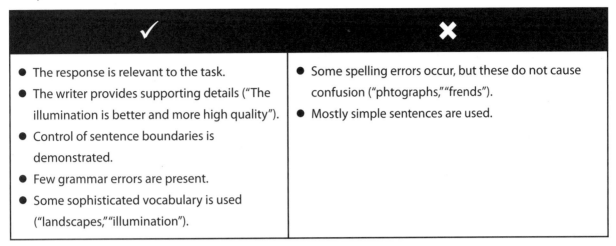

✓	✗
• The response is relevant to the task. • The writer provides supporting details ("The illumination is better and more high quality"). • Control of sentence boundaries is demonstrated. • Few grammar errors are present. • Some sophisticated vocabulary is used ("landscapes," "illumination").	• Some spelling errors occur, but these do not cause confusion ("phtographs," "frends"). • Mostly simple sentences are used.

CEFR Level: B2

Task 2:

Some public places have a lot of garbage. One solution is to provide more trash cans for people to use. Another option is to increase penalties for people who throw garbage on the street. What do you think should be done? Use specific examples to support your opinion.

In my opinion, first of all, we have to invest in education because people who throw garbage on the street does not have education, a thing that is essential and cames of the parents to.

I agree with increase penalties for people who throw garbage on the street because it looks like they can not put in their bags or pockets and wait to find a trash to throw, but I understand that sometimes people are not carring bags or have a pocket to put away, so I agree with provide more trash cans for people to use to. With more trash cans, less floods we will have, I guess.

But all of this requires invest, so it is not a thing that we can do by ourselfs, the government have to do their part to help the environment, the nature, help us to have a clean city with no trash, no pollution.

For all of this, things works, we have to become aware for all the problems that around us and help and do what we can.

Writing Test Responses Commentary

Commentary:

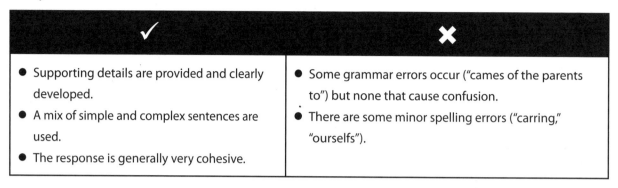

✓	✗
• Supporting details are provided and clearly developed. • A mix of simple and complex sentences are used. • The response is generally very cohesive.	• Some grammar errors occur ("cames of the parents to") but none that cause confusion. • There are some minor spelling errors ("carring," "ourselfs").

CEFR Level: C1

Task 1:

1. **Do you like to take photographs? What do you take photographs of?**

   I really like taking photographs and I usually photograph plants or landscapes.

2. **Describe a place where you like to take photographs.**

   I like taking photographs and the beach, moutans and sometimes at my city's parks.

3. **Tell us about a photograph you took recently.**

   The last photograph I took was last week and there was a palm tree in a sunshining day. The sky was blue and it looked very bright.

Commentary:

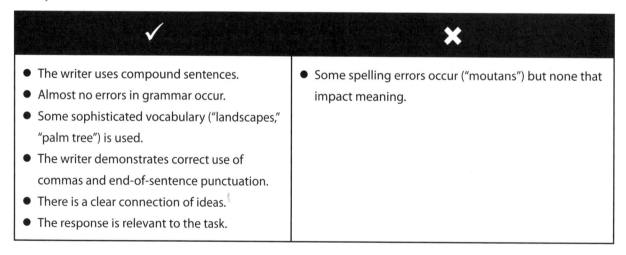

✓	✗
• The writer uses compound sentences. • Almost no errors in grammar occur. • Some sophisticated vocabulary ("landscapes," "palm tree") is used. • The writer demonstrates correct use of commas and end-of-sentence punctuation. • There is a clear connection of ideas. • The response is relevant to the task.	• Some spelling errors occur ("moutans") but none that impact meaning.

CEFR Level: C1

Task 2:

Some public places have a lot of garbage. One solution is to provide more trash cans for people to use. Another option is to increase penalties for people who throw garbage on the street. What do you think should be done? Use specific examples to support your opinion.

As the world seems to be a little more dirty every day, solutions for these problems must be talked about. Providing more trash cans and increasing penalitis for thrown garbage on the street are both good solutions that might help our planet in this point. But if we want it to be very significant, we cannot just choose one of them; they have to be put in action together, then we can get better results.

A lot of times I saw myself holding my rubbish for a long time because there were not trash cans where I could throw it away and I am sure that it did not happen just to me. People get tired of holding these stuff so long, so they just drop it. It does not seem so bad, but it can cause so many floods, animals death because of eating and pollution is general. If we put more trash cans, people will not have problems about dropping the garbage in the right place because it will be very close to them.

In our society, putting the rubbish in the adequate place is, mostly, a moral "rule". People are told since they are children that doing this is good for the environment. None the less, as they are not punished, they keep doing what is easier for them (in this case, not holding the garbage in their hands). Considering it, increasing penalties is a good option because then, people have more to lose than just a clean place to live (and it really hurts).

Even though the penalties are a good option, it does not work so good alone. Some cities in Brazil, like Rio de Janiero, are examples; the penalties were increased and the level of pollution decreased but it was not enough, considering the amount of trash. So, in my opinion, the solutions are good and can make things better, but if we want bigger results, we should increase both together.

Commentary:

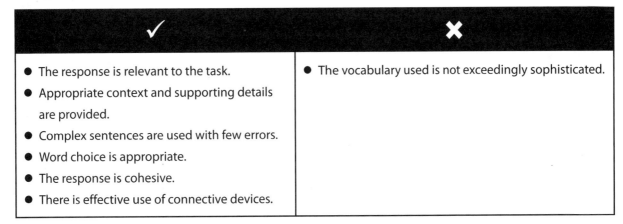

✓	✗
• The response is relevant to the task. • Appropriate context and supporting details are provided. • Complex sentences are used with few errors. • Word choice is appropriate. • The response is cohesive. • There is effective use of connective devices.	• The vocabulary used is not exceedingly sophisticated.

Examiner Instructions and Script

The examiner script provided should be used with every test-taker to ensure a consistent testing experience for all. The information in normal text is to be read aloud. You will need a stopwatch. **The information in italics explains what you, as examiner, should do.** We recommend you record the responses for evaluation purposes.

Examiner to Test-Taker — Part 1

- Welcome to the MET Speaking Test. My name is _____, and I'll be giving you the test.
- What is your name?

Wait for the answer.

- Would you spell your name please?

Write down the test-taker's name on the scoring sheet.

- Thank you, _____.

Say the test-taker's name.

- This test has 5 tasks and lasts about 10 minutes.
- The tasks are printed on the test card. I'll also read them aloud to you.
- There are no right or wrong answers on this test. Be sure to say as much as you can in the time allowed. I will tell you when your time is up.
- Before we begin, do you have any questions?
- Now we are going to start the first part of the test.

Hand out the test card (see page XXX). Part 1 faces up.

- In this part of the test, you will describe a picture and complete some tasks.

Read aloud Task 1; point to the image.
Start the stopwatch. After 60 seconds have elapsed, say:

- Thank you.

Read aloud Task 2. Start the stopwatch.
After 60 seconds have elapsed, say:

- Thank you.

Read aloud Task 3. Start the stopwatch.
After 60 seconds have elapsed, say:

- Thank you.
- Now, please turn your test card over and read the directions to Part 2**.**

Examiner to Test-Taker — Part 2

- Let's begin.

Read aloud Task 4.
Start the stopwatch.
After 90 seconds have elapsed, say:

- Thank you.

Read aloud Task 5.
Start the stopwatch.
After 90 seconds have elapsed, say:

- Thank you.

Collect the test card.

- This is the end of the MET Speaking Test. Thank you.

Test Taker's Card

Part 1

Directions

In this part of the test, you will describe a picture and complete some tasks.

| Task 1 | *60 seconds* |

Describe the beach.

Speaking Prompt

| Task 2 | *60 seconds* |

Tell me about what you do when you relax outside.

| Task 3 | *60 seconds* |

Some people think spending time outside helps us relax and stay healthy. How do you feel after you spend time outside? Explain your answer.

Prompts for Test 1

TASK 4. [90 seconds]

Your friend is thinking about leaving college so he can play music full-time. He wants to take time to travel with his rock band while he is still young. What are the advantages and disadvantages of this idea?

TASK 5. [90 seconds]

The number of students at a local school has grown. Some teachers have suggested moving the students to a new school to solve this problem. Many parents think this is a bad idea. I am the school principal. Tell me what you think about this idea and try to convince me to agree with you.

Speaking Test

Part 1

Directions

In this part of the test, you will describe a picture and complete some tasks.

Task 1	*60 seconds*

Describe the sporting event.

Speaking Prompt

Task 2	*60 seconds*

Tell me about a time when you watched a sporting event.

Task 3	*60 seconds*

Some people enjoy playing team sports. Others prefer to simply exercise by themselves. Which do you prefer? Give your opinion and reasons to support it.

Prompts for Test 2

TASK 4. [90 seconds]

A friend of yours wants to get a second college degree and would like your advice. Your friend is considering attending a small local school instead of an expensive, well-known university. What are the advantages and disadvantages of this idea?

TASK 5. [90 seconds]

The principal at the local high school is considering adding cooking classes to replace some traditional science classes. She wants to educate all young people about eating healthy food. I am a member of the school board. Tell me what you think about this idea and try to convince me to agree with you.

Test Taker's Card

Part 1

Directions

In this part of the test, you will describe a picture and complete some tasks.

| Task 1 | *60 seconds* |

Describe the airport.

| Task 2 | *60 seconds* |

Tell me about the last time you traveled somewhere.

| Task 3 | *60 seconds* |

Some people like traveling. Other people prefer to stay home. How do you feel about traveling? Give your opinion and reasons to support it.

Speaking Prompt

Prompts for Test 3

TASK 4. [90 seconds]

My town is hosting a music festival this spring. Many university students would like to work at the festival. What are the advantages and disadvantages of hiring students to do this work?

TASK 5. [90 seconds]

To improve teenagers' health, the school board wants to add mandatory exercise classes every day. Some people think this is a bad idea because there would be less time for other subjects. I work for the school board. Tell me what you think about this proposal and convince me to agree with you.

Test Taker's Card

Part 1

Directions

In this part of the test, you will describe a picture and complete some tasks.

| Task 1 | *60 seconds* |

Describe the family meal.

| Task 2 | *60 seconds* |

Tell me about a meal that you really enjoyed.

| Task 3 | *60 seconds* |

Some people like to eat at home. Other people like to go to restaurants. What do you prefer to do? Give your opinion and reasons to support it.

Speaking Prompt

Prompts for Test 4

TASK 4. [90 seconds]

The local education board is thinking of reducing the hours that children spend in school from 7 hours a day to 4 hours a day in order to save money. What are the advantages and disadvantages of this idea?

TASK 5. [90 seconds]

Parents in your community want to become involved in their children's education. They want to teach in the schools even though they don't have teaching experience. Some teachers do not like this idea. I'm a member of the school board. Tell me what you think about this and try to convince me to agree with you.

MET General Instructions

Look only at your own test. Examinees giving or receiving answers or using notes or other aids will be disqualified, and they will fail. Examination fees will not be refunded.

Look at the TOP RIGHT of SIDE ONE of your answer sheet. Fill in the following information on the lines:

- **FULL NAME:** print your full name in this order: family name, then first name, then middle initial (MI). Use all capital letters.
- **YOUR SIGNATURE:** sign your name.
- **TEST CENTER:** print the name of the city in which you are taking this test.
- **NATIVE LANGUAGE:** print your native language.
- **TODAY'S DATE:** print the month, day, and year.

Look at the TOP LEFT of SIDE ONE of your answer sheet. Use capital letters to fill in the following information in the blocks. Use the same spelling you used on your registration form:

- **LAST NAME:** print your main family name in the blocks, one letter per block. There are 13 blocks. If your last name is longer than 13 letters, print only the first 13 letters.
- **FIRST:** print the first 6 letters of your first name.
- **MI:** print the initial of your middle name.

Look at the columns of CIRCLES BELOW THE BLOCKS:

- Find the letter that is the same as the letter you have printed in the block above.
- Darken the circle completely so that you cannot see the letter inside.
- Do this for all the letters of your last name, first name, and middle initial.
- Darken only one circle in each of the columns.

Look at the BOTTOM LEFT of SIDE ONE of your answer sheet.

- **BIRTHDATE:** find the month you were born and darken the circle next to it.
- **DAY:** print the day you were born. If it is a 1-digit day, write zero first. Darken the circles underneath these numbers.
- **YEAR:** print the last two digits of the year you were born. Darken the circles underneath these numbers.
- **GENDER:** darken the circle "M" (male) or "F" (female).
- **LANG. (Language):** print the 2-digit code number for your native language (the examiner will tell you the number). Darken the circles.
- **CENTER NO.:** print the 3-digit test center number (the examiner will tell you the number). Darken the circles.
- **REG. NO.:** print your 6-digit personal registration number. Include all zeros, including those at the beginning of the number. Darken the circles.
- **FORM:** darken the circle for the form letter of this test. Make sure the letter you darken matches the form letter on the cover of this test booklet.

This test will be machine scored, so you must follow instructions carefully:

- Do not bend or fold your answer sheet.
- Mark all your answers on the separate answer sheet. Answers marked in the booklet will not be scored.
- Use a number 2 (soft) pencil.
- Your mark must be dark enough to be read by the scanning machine. The scanner cannot see very light marks.
- Do not make any other marks on your answer sheet.
- If you change your mind about an answer, erase your first mark completely.
- Fill in only one circle for each question.
- Any question with more than one answer marked will be counted wrong.
- If you are not sure about an answer, you may guess.

When instructed to, look through the rest of the test booklet to see that it is complete. Check the pages quickly. You should have 23 numbered pages in your test booklet. If there are pages missing from your booklet, raise your hand and a proctor will give you a replacement.

Listening Section Instructions

In this section of the test, you will show your ability to understand spoken English. There are three parts in this section, with special directions for each part.

Mark all your answers on the separate answer sheet. Do not make any stray marks on the answer sheet. If you change your mind about an answer, erase your first answer completely. If you do not know the answer, you may guess. Try to answer as many questions as possible.

Part 1

In this part of the test, you will hear short conversations between two people. After each conversation, you will hear a question about it. Choose the best answer to the question from the choices printed in the test booklet, and mark your answer on the separate answer sheet. You should mark A, B, C, or D.

There are 19 questions in Part 1. The conversations and questions will not be repeated. Please listen carefully.

Part 2

In this part of the test, you will hear longer conversations between two people. After each conversation, you will answer some questions about it. Choose the best answer to the question from the choices printed in the test booklet, and mark your answer on the separate answer sheet. You should mark A, B, C, or D.

There are 14 questions in Part 2. The conversations and questions will not be repeated. If you want to, you may take notes in your booklet as you listen. Please listen carefully.

Part 3

In this part, you will hear some short talks. After each talk, you will answer some questions about it. Choose the best answer to the question from the choices printed in the test booklet, and mark your answer on the separate answer sheet. You should mark A, B, C, or D.

There are 17 questions in Part 3. The talks and questions will not be repeated. If you want to, you may take notes in your booklet as you listen. Please listen carefully.

Reading and Grammar Section Instructions

This section of the test focuses on your ability to use English grammar and to understand written English. There are 50 questions in this part of the test. They are numbered 51 to 100.

You will have 65 minutes to complete the entire section. Try to answer all questions. You may answer the questions in any order you wish.

Each question has only one correct answer. Choose the best answer to the question from the choices printed in the test booklet, and mark your answer on side 2 of the separate answer sheet. You should mark A, B, C, or D. Do not make any stray marks on your answer sheet. If you change your mind about an answer, erase your first mark completely. If you are not sure about an answer, you may guess.

You may begin now.

Writing Section Instructions

This writing test has two parts: Task 1 is on the back of this booklet and Task 2 is inside this booklet.
- You have 45 minutes to complete both parts.
- Your responses to both parts should be written in this booklet.
- You will not be graded on the appearance of your paper, but your handwriting must be readable. You may change or correct your writing, but you should not recopy your entire response.
1. Fill in your name, signature, ID number, and today's date in the box above. They must exactly match the information on your registration form.
2. When the examiner tells you to, turn your booklet over and begin Task 1.
3. When you are done with Task 1, open your booklet and continue on to Task 2.

Do not turn your booklet over until the examiner tells you to.

MET
LISTENING
& READING

Full Name (PRINT)

Today's Date
(mm/dd/yy)

Signature

REGISTRATION

⓪	⓪	⓪	⓪	⓪	⓪
①	①	①	①	①	①
②	②	②	②	②	②
③	③	③	③	③	③
④	④	④	④	④	④
⑤	⑤	⑤	⑤	⑤	⑤
⑥	⑥	⑥	⑥	⑥	⑥
⑦	⑦	⑦	⑦	⑦	⑦
⑧	⑧	⑧	⑧	⑧	⑧
⑨	⑨	⑨	⑨	⑨	⑨

CENTER

⓪	⓪	⓪
①	①	①
②	②	②
③	③	③
④	④	④
⑤	⑤	⑤
⑥	⑥	⑥
⑦	⑦	⑦
⑧	⑧	⑧
⑨	⑨	⑨

LAN

⓪	⓪
①	①
②	②
③	③
④	④
⑤	⑤
⑥	⑥
⑦	⑦
⑧	⑧
⑨	⑨

GENDER

Ⓜ MALE
Ⓕ FEMALE

FORM

Ⓐ FORM A
Ⓑ FORM B

T0000021

MET
LISTENING & READING

REGISTRATION

Full Name (PRINT)

LISTENING

1. Ⓐ Ⓑ Ⓒ Ⓓ   14. Ⓐ Ⓑ Ⓒ Ⓓ   27. Ⓐ Ⓑ Ⓒ Ⓓ   40. Ⓐ Ⓑ Ⓒ Ⓓ
2. Ⓐ Ⓑ Ⓒ Ⓓ   15. Ⓐ Ⓑ Ⓒ Ⓓ   28. Ⓐ Ⓑ Ⓒ Ⓓ   41. Ⓐ Ⓑ Ⓒ Ⓓ
3. Ⓐ Ⓑ Ⓒ Ⓓ   16. Ⓐ Ⓑ Ⓒ Ⓓ   29. Ⓐ Ⓑ Ⓒ Ⓓ   42. Ⓐ Ⓑ Ⓒ Ⓓ
4. Ⓐ Ⓑ Ⓒ Ⓓ   17. Ⓐ Ⓑ Ⓒ Ⓓ   30. Ⓐ Ⓑ Ⓒ Ⓓ   43. Ⓐ Ⓑ Ⓒ Ⓓ
5. Ⓐ Ⓑ Ⓒ Ⓓ   18. Ⓐ Ⓑ Ⓒ Ⓓ   31. Ⓐ Ⓑ Ⓒ Ⓓ   44. Ⓐ Ⓑ Ⓒ Ⓓ
6. Ⓐ Ⓑ Ⓒ Ⓓ   19. Ⓐ Ⓑ Ⓒ Ⓓ   32. Ⓐ Ⓑ Ⓒ Ⓓ   45. Ⓐ Ⓑ Ⓒ Ⓓ
7. Ⓐ Ⓑ Ⓒ Ⓓ   20. Ⓐ Ⓑ Ⓒ Ⓓ   33. Ⓐ Ⓑ Ⓒ Ⓓ   46. Ⓐ Ⓑ Ⓒ Ⓓ
8. Ⓐ Ⓑ Ⓒ Ⓓ   21. Ⓐ Ⓑ Ⓒ Ⓓ   34. Ⓐ Ⓑ Ⓒ Ⓓ   47. Ⓐ Ⓑ Ⓒ Ⓓ
9. Ⓐ Ⓑ Ⓒ Ⓓ   22. Ⓐ Ⓑ Ⓒ Ⓓ   35. Ⓐ Ⓑ Ⓒ Ⓓ   48. Ⓐ Ⓑ Ⓒ Ⓓ
10. Ⓐ Ⓑ Ⓒ Ⓓ   23. Ⓐ Ⓑ Ⓒ Ⓓ   36. Ⓐ Ⓑ Ⓒ Ⓓ   49. Ⓐ Ⓑ Ⓒ Ⓓ
11. Ⓐ Ⓑ Ⓒ Ⓓ   24. Ⓐ Ⓑ Ⓒ Ⓓ   37. Ⓐ Ⓑ Ⓒ Ⓓ   50. Ⓐ Ⓑ Ⓒ Ⓓ
12. Ⓐ Ⓑ Ⓒ Ⓓ   25. Ⓐ Ⓑ Ⓒ Ⓓ   38. Ⓐ Ⓑ Ⓒ Ⓓ
13. Ⓐ Ⓑ Ⓒ Ⓓ   26. Ⓐ Ⓑ Ⓒ Ⓓ   39. Ⓐ Ⓑ Ⓒ Ⓓ

READING

51. Ⓐ Ⓑ Ⓒ Ⓓ   64. Ⓐ Ⓑ Ⓒ Ⓓ   77. Ⓐ Ⓑ Ⓒ Ⓓ   90. Ⓐ Ⓑ Ⓒ Ⓓ
52. Ⓐ Ⓑ Ⓒ Ⓓ   65. Ⓐ Ⓑ Ⓒ Ⓓ   78. Ⓐ Ⓑ Ⓒ Ⓓ   91. Ⓐ Ⓑ Ⓒ Ⓓ
53. Ⓐ Ⓑ Ⓒ Ⓓ   66. Ⓐ Ⓑ Ⓒ Ⓓ   79. Ⓐ Ⓑ Ⓒ Ⓓ   92. Ⓐ Ⓑ Ⓒ Ⓓ
54. Ⓐ Ⓑ Ⓒ Ⓓ   67. Ⓐ Ⓑ Ⓒ Ⓓ   80. Ⓐ Ⓑ Ⓒ Ⓓ   93. Ⓐ Ⓑ Ⓒ Ⓓ
55. Ⓐ Ⓑ Ⓒ Ⓓ   68. Ⓐ Ⓑ Ⓒ Ⓓ   81. Ⓐ Ⓑ Ⓒ Ⓓ   94. Ⓐ Ⓑ Ⓒ Ⓓ
56. Ⓐ Ⓑ Ⓒ Ⓓ   69. Ⓐ Ⓑ Ⓒ Ⓓ   82. Ⓐ Ⓑ Ⓒ Ⓓ   95. Ⓐ Ⓑ Ⓒ Ⓓ
57. Ⓐ Ⓑ Ⓒ Ⓓ   70. Ⓐ Ⓑ Ⓒ Ⓓ   83. Ⓐ Ⓑ Ⓒ Ⓓ   96. Ⓐ Ⓑ Ⓒ Ⓓ
58. Ⓐ Ⓑ Ⓒ Ⓓ   71. Ⓐ Ⓑ Ⓒ Ⓓ   84. Ⓐ Ⓑ Ⓒ Ⓓ   97. Ⓐ Ⓑ Ⓒ Ⓓ
59. Ⓐ Ⓑ Ⓒ Ⓓ   72. Ⓐ Ⓑ Ⓒ Ⓓ   85. Ⓐ Ⓑ Ⓒ Ⓓ   98. Ⓐ Ⓑ Ⓒ Ⓓ
60. Ⓐ Ⓑ Ⓒ Ⓓ   73. Ⓐ Ⓑ Ⓒ Ⓓ   86. Ⓐ Ⓑ Ⓒ Ⓓ   99. Ⓐ Ⓑ Ⓒ Ⓓ
61. Ⓐ Ⓑ Ⓒ Ⓓ   74. Ⓐ Ⓑ Ⓒ Ⓓ   87. Ⓐ Ⓑ Ⓒ Ⓓ   100. Ⓐ Ⓑ Ⓒ Ⓓ
62. Ⓐ Ⓑ Ⓒ Ⓓ   75. Ⓐ Ⓑ Ⓒ Ⓓ   88. Ⓐ Ⓑ Ⓒ Ⓓ
63. Ⓐ Ⓑ Ⓒ Ⓓ   76. Ⓐ Ⓑ Ⓒ Ⓓ   89. Ⓐ Ⓑ Ⓒ Ⓓ